The Poetry of Ignazio Buttitta

Legas

Pueti D'Arba Sicula Series

Volume XIX

Series Editor: Gaetano Cipolla

Other Volumes Published in this Series:

Volume I- Vincenzo Ancona, *Maliditttu la lingua/Damned Language*, edited by Anna Chairetakis and Joseph Sciorra, translated into English by Gaetano Cipolla, 1990;
Volume II- *The Poetry of Nino Martoglio*, edited, introduced and translated by Gaetano Cipolla, 1993;
Volume III- Giovanni Meli, *Moral Fables and Other Poems*, edited, introduced and translated by Gaetano Cipolla, 1995;
Volume IV- Antonino Provenzano, *Vinissi/I'd Love to Come...*, edited and translated by Gaetano Cipolla, 1995;
Volume V- *Sicilian Erotica,* edited and translated by Onat Claypole, introduction by Justin Vitiello, 1997.
Volume VI- Giovanni Meli, *Don Chisciotti and Sanciu Panza,* edited, introduced and translated by Gaetano Cipolla, 2003.
Volume VII- Antonio Veneziano, *Ninety Love Octaves*, edited, introduced and translated by Gaetano Cipolla, 2007.
Volume VIII- Antonino Provenzano, *Tornu / The Return,* translated by Gaetano Cipolla, 2009.
Volume IX- Domenico Tempio, *Poems and Fables*, introduced and translated by Giovanna Summerfield, 2010.
Volume X- Senzio Mazza, *Pizzini d'amuri / Love Notes*, Introduction and translated by Gaetano Cipolla, 2012.
Volume XI- Salvatore Di Marco, *L'aranciu amaru e autri puisii / The Bitter Orange and Other Poems*, translated by Gaetano Cipolla, 2013.
Volume XII- Nino De Vita, *The Poetry of Nino De Vita*, translated by Gaetano Cipolla, 2014
Volume XIII- Piero Carbone, *Lu pueta parra pi tutti / The Poets Speaks for All,* introduced and translated by Gaetano Cipolla, 2014.
Volume XIV- *The Poetry of Giovanni Meli*, edited, introduced and translated by Gaetano Cipolla, 2015.
Volume XV- Antonino Provenzano, *Pirati supra la nivi /Footprints in the Snow,* translated by Gaetano Cipolla, 2016.
Volume XVI- Maria Nivea Zagarella, *The poetry of Maria Nivea Zagarella*, edited, introduced and translated by Gaetano Cipolla, 2020.
Volume XVII- Giovanni Meli, *Giovanni Meli: Social Critic*, edited, introduced and translated by Gaetano Cipolla, 2020.
XVIII- Antonio Veneziano, Sicilian *Rhymes of Love, Disdain, and Faith*, Edited, introduced and translated by Gaetano Cipolla, 2020.

Ignazio Buttitta

The Poetry of Ignazio Buttitta

Edited, introduced and translated into English verse
by Gaetano Cipolla

The Poetry of Ignazio Buttitta, (a Bilingual Anthology, Sicilian/English), edited, introduced and translated into English verse by Gaetano Cipolla.
ISBN 978-1-939693-49-5
Library of Congress Control Number: 2023936431

Acknowledgements

I gratefully acknowledge a generous grant to Arba Sicula by Salvatore Liotta that made it possible to print enough copies to mail to all the members of the organization free of charge. We are grateful to Salvatore who made this donation in memory of his Sicilian grandfather, Salvatore Liotta.

I also want to express my gratitude to Emanuele and Ignazio Buttitta and the Buttitta Foundation for providing me with copies in PDF of all the works published by Ignazio Buttitta. I would not have been able to complete this volume without them. I am also indebted to Marco Scalabrino whose *Ignazio Buttitta: dalla piazza all'universo*, provided a wealth of critical appraisals of Buttitta's career as a poet and to Salvatore Di Marco whose extensive scholarship is a must for those who want to learn more about Buttitta's place in the Sicilian poetry of the past century. I also want to thank the artist Carlo Puleo who was a good friend to Buttitta and often accompanied the poet when he traveled to speak at gatherings in different Sicilian towns. We thank him for the use of his rendition of Buttitta addressing the crowd and for his story about the poet, published in *Arba Sicula*. I am grateful to Giuseppe Quatriglio and Justin Vitiello, both of whom are no longer with us, and to Maria Zagarella for her two articles on Buttitta, as well as to all those who are listed in the bibliography who provided valuable insights to understand the work of this poet who devoted his whole life to "removing thorns and planting roses" in the garden of Sicily. Buttitta with this volume speaks his message of peace, freedom and brotherhood to the English-speaking world.

for information and order write to:

Legas

P. O. Box 149
Mineola, NY 11501
USA

3 Wood Aster Bay
Ottawa, ONTARIO
K2R ID3

Legasbooks2021@outlook.com

Indice / Tble of Contents

Ignazio Buttitta, *Il poeta in piazza*, painting by Carlo Puleo

Introduction

I begin this introduction with a confession. I eulogized Ignazio Buttitta twice: once when he was still alive and another when he passed away in 1997. One night while working on something the RAI Television program was on as background noise, but at one point I heard the announcer say the name Buttitta and gave details about a funeral. I did not hear the first name but knowing that Buttitta was already in his eighties, I assumed they were referring to Ignazio Buttitta who was for Arba Sicula a very important poet. His nearly exclusive use of the Sicilian language in his work and his passionate defense of it in the poem "Lingua e dialettu" had made him one of the pillars on which Arba Si- cula stood. In fact, his poem was published in the first issue of the *Arba Sicula Review* in 1979. The poem, included in this anthology, laments the fact that Sicilian "is losing a chord every day" ("perdi na corda ogni jornu") and states categorically that a people become poor and enslaved when they are robbed of the language they inherited from their forefathers. The words of this poem are like the national anthem for Arba Sicula, an organization that was founded to study, preserve, and disseminate the language and culture of Sicily. As President, I could not let the death of Ignazio Buttitta pass without commemorating him and his work in some tangible way. So I prepared a special section in our *Sicilia Parra* newsletter announcing his passing and reprinting "Lingua e dialettu," together with a selection of other poems. After copies of the newsletter arrived in Sicily, my good friend Giuseppe Quatriglio called me to ask me where I had heard the news that Buttitta had died. To my chagrin, he told me that the poet was alive and well. The Buttitta who had passed away was one of his sons, Pietro Buttitta. You can imagine my embarrassment, but fortunately for me nobody else read or understood the article in Sicily. *Sicilia Parra* is written in English, unlike *Arba Sicula* which has a bilingual format: Sicilian/English).

The second commemoration of Buttitta's life came after he passed away for real on April 5th 1997. I made sure, of course, that the information was correct. He was 97 years old. A special section of *Arba Sicula,* dedicated to him in volume XVII, published in 1997, contained an interesting report by Alfio Patti on how Buttitta lived and worked in his house in Aspra, together with an ample selection of his poems translated by Justin Vitiello. But even before that issue, *Arba Sicula* had devoted another special section to Buttitta with a wonderful appraisal of his work by Giuseppe Quatriglio, and a sizable selections of poems with my translation this time.

Our long-standing relationship with the poet entitles us to be the first to present an anthology of his work to the English-speaking world. We have shared not only his passionate defense of the Sicilian language but also his defense of the poor people of Sicily who have struggled hard under foreign dominations, who have been forced to emigrate to different countries to find a more decent way to live and to sustain their families, who have been denied the right to work, ever bowing before the powerful, while suffering hunger and disease. We have shared his regret for the prejudices that have accompanied the good Sicilian people for centuries, for the stigma of the Mafia that has tarnished our reputations, for the belief that Sicilians speak a mongrel language when, in fact, it was the first Italic language, emerging from Latin, worthy to be used in poetry. For these reasons, it is a privilege for me to lend Buttitta my English voice as I prepare this anthology that is volume XIX of the Series "Pueti of Arba Sicula" (Poets of Arba Sicula) a series that I founded on the belief that poets are the best ambassadors of a country. And it is an interesting coincidence that the first volume of the series was *Malidittu la lingua/Damned Language*, by Vincenzo Ancona, the poet from Castellammare del Golfo who emigrated to Brooklyn and became a beloved bard for the Sicilian community in New York, much like Buttitta was a much loved poet not only in Bagheria, but all of Sicily and beyond the borders of Italy, as well. He traveled to Russia, to France and other countries and performed before enthusiastic crowds in many places. And it is not a coincidence that when I went to Bagheria to visit Buttitta I brought him a copy of Ancona's book. I published a picture of myself standing with the book in my hand between Buttitta and his wife Angelina who were seated in front of their store in Bagheria. These two poets share many similarities. They belong to a category of old school poets who learned their craft by themselves without going to school. And they were both poets who had the power to mesmerize an audience. Ancona, who could recite his poetry for hours without ever looking at a sheet of paper, did for the Arba Sicula crowd and for the Castellammaresi in New York, what Buttitta did for a much wider audience that stretched across Europe. And while I never had the privilege of being present at Buttitta's performances, I have seen videos where he recites from memory. Giuseppe Quatriglio, who knew the poet very well, described Buttitta's relationship with the crowd:

> "His vitality was absolutely remarkable, as was his way of being present on the stage of the world; a presence that was charged and stimulated by contact with a crowd. Ignazio Buttitta was an authentic street poet who was able to transfigure things before a crowd assembled to listen to him. He breathed then in a wider atmosphere, the images

flew acquiring fantastic dimensions, but his tone was sharp and precise in making moral judgements, in condemning, in accusing, in affirming a higher truth. Ignazio Buttitta was a cosmic entity... Ignazio Buttitta knew how to move people and be knew how to surprise through his exemplary social and human presence, for his ability to give a universal dimension to passions, to anguish and to the questions of our time, for his clear-sighted interpretation of the malaise or our society."

I like to think that it was not just his voice and his ability as a performer that mesmerized the crowd. I like to think that it was the power of the Sicilian language that moved people, by reawakening in them things that had been dormant for many years, bringing back images and feelings that the modern age has erased or sent below the level of consciousness. If I may, I would like to illustrate this with something that happened to me. In 1995, I was invited to London by a large association of Sicilians who lived in England, the Trinacria Association. I was to receive the "Man of the Year Award" for my activities on behalf of Sicilian language and culture. At the Gala banquet there were about 700 Sicilians in the hotel ballroom. As happens whenever so many Sicilians get together, they cannot stop talking to their friends and acquaintances. The chatter was deafening and when the presentations began, the organizers had to speak over the chatter. Important guests were there: the Archbishop of Palermo, Franco Zeffirelli, the famous director, and others and their speeches were drowned by the chatter, so much so that Zeffirelli was highly offended and stopped talking.

I began to panic. If the crowd paid no attention to such important people, what would they do when I was introduced? Disaster loomed in my mind, but when they finally introduced me, I mumbled some words of thanks and then I began reciting Buttitta's famous poem "Lingua e dialettu":

Un populu	A people
mittitilu a catina	put them in chains
spugghiatilu,	strip them naked
attuppatici	plug up
a vucca,	their mouths
è ancora libiru.	are still free.
Livatici u travagghiu	Take away their work
u passaportu,	their passports,
a tavula unni mancia,	the table where they eat,
u lettu unni dormi,	the bed where they sleep,

è ancora riccu.	they are still rich.
Un populu	A people
diventa poviru e servu	become poor and enslaved
quannu ci arrobbanu a lingua	when you rob them of their language,
addutata dî patri:	inherited from their forefathers:
è persu pi sempri.	they are lost forever.

By the time I recited the second quartet, things had quieted down and by the next quartet, you could hear a pin drop in that crowded ballroom. I was able to recite the poem in full to an audience whose mood had changed miraculously. I do not attribute the change to my abilities as a speaker, but to the power of the Sicilian language that, if you are Sicilian, reaches into your stomach and touches your unconscious. It is the power of poetry that I discovered when I read the poem by Giovanni Meli that begins with

Ucchiuzzi niuri	Black lovely eyes
si taliati	if you look coy
faciti cadiri	houses and cities
casi e citati.	you will destroy

The first line, "Ucchiuzzi niuri," reached my soul viscerally, something that does not happen if I translate the line into Italian. "Occhiucci neri" does not have the same effect on me. Why? Because "ucchiuzzi niuri" awakens memories of childhood when Sicilian for me and for all Sicilians of a certain age, was the language learned on our mother's lap: the language of the heart. We all learned Italian in school as a second language. Antonio Veneziano, the greatest Sicilian poet of the Renaissance, a poet who wrote only in Sicilian because he did not want to become a parrot mouthing the language of others, said it best: "A great emotion cannot be better expressed than in the mother's language."

Ignazio Buttitta knew this very well. The Sicilian language was for him the essential medium through which he could identify with the people who breathed and dreamed in Sicilian. He adopted the Sicilian language because it was and is the language of the people, even though he realized that it was losing "a chord every day." And like the great poets of the past, he did not use the dialect of the town where he was born (Bagheria), but a language that can be understood by all Sicilians, rich and poor, illiterate and well educated, peasant and nobility. His poetry was expressed in the language of the Sicilian people. And this is not true only for the language that he used. It is a feature that embraces the emotional universe of the Sicilian people, their sense of justice, their condemnation of injustice, their longing for peace, their hatred for war, and their longing for equality and freedom. His poetry is an embrace of the have nots, the homeless, the poor, expressed in a way that is accessible to everyone. His themes cover the gamut of emotions, all readily accessible to everyone. Let us review some of the major themes as represented by some of his iconic poems:

The poem "Letter to a German Mother," is not only an emotional condemnation of war but a confession of his own guilt for having participated in it. The letter asks the German mother to forgive him for having killed her son during the First World War. When he accepted the Mondello Prize, many years after the event, Buttitta recited this poem, but before doing so, he explained that as a seventeen year old machine gunner, Buttitta shot the German soldier. He carried his guilt for many years. So much so that in the poem "I petri niuri" ("The Black Stones"), published in 1983, which was his last book, he recalled the event. He had been writing about a man who had committed two murders and asked: "How many times a murderer am I? / I'm at the Piave River, / Advancing / shooting /killing: / I'm at the Piave River / I'm fighting with a bayonet, / I'm disemboweling men, / I'm stepping over them, / and all like me: / animals and people / enemies and Italians / daring and cowardly / infidels and baptized / in hell and paradise, / on altars and on gallows: / all of them like me!... / all murderers like me!..."

The second poem that reflects an important aspect of Buttitta's work as a militant poet engaged in the struggle for equality and a better treatment for the working class is entitled "Lamentu pi la morti di Turiddu Carnivali," ("Lament for the Death of Turiddu Carnivali") in which he presented the story of a Socialist union organizer who was killed by the Mafia on May 16, 1955. In the poem that consists of 21 rhymed octaves that combine lyricism and drama, Buttitta transformed the murdered organizer into a larger-than-life figure, almost a mythological figure that shares many similarities with Jesus Christ. In fact, the poem makes ample use of symbolism connected with the passion and death of Jesus Christ. In the first octave, the poet sets the stage by calling Turiddu an angel who made miracles and by saying that like Christ he too died at the hands of murderers:

> Ancilu era e non avìa ali
> non era santu e miraculi facìa,
> ncelu acchianava senza cordi e scali
> e senza appidamenti nni scinnìa;
> era l'amuri lu sò capitali
> e sta ricchizza a tutti la spartìa:
> Turiddu Carnivali nnuminatu
> e comu Cristu murìu ammazzatu.

He was an angel and he had no wings,
was not a saint, yet he made miracles.
He rose to heaven without ropes or stairs;
and he climbed down without supports.
Love was the capital that he possessed,
and all this wealth he shared with everyone.
Turiddu Carnivali was his name.
Christ's murder and Turiddu's were the same.

Turiddu himself, while talking to his mother after his confrontation with the police, went home with a somber look on his face. He knew what would happen and he said to his grieving mother "Mother, my day has come," and then he sighed; "They murdered Christ, but he was innocent." The connection with Christ is underlined by the poet. When describing the conversation between Turiddu and his mother, he stopped his narration and asked his listeners to raise their voices against the injustice, "You people standing here, shout for the loss!" and added that in his mother's eyes, Turiddu had met the same fate as Christ: "His mother saw her son dead on the cross." And Turiddu's mother, unlike the Madonna who is nearly always shown in a semiconscious state, vanquished by her pain and sorrow, behaved like a true Sicilian mother, running wildly through the streets, acting like the professional mourners that were once hired to mourn the dead in Sicily, except that the sorrow she expressed was real, not a performance:

Gridava, figghiu pi strati e vaneddi
la strangusciata matri chi currìa
pi la trazzera a stramazzamareddi:
un fasciu di sarmenti chi svampia
dintra d'un furnu e ventu a li spurteddi:
"Curriti tutti a chiànciri cu mia!
Puvireddi, nisciti di li tani,
morsi ammazzatu pi lu vostru pani!"

The mother, screaming for her son, just whirred
through streets and alleyways in desperation,
running haphazardly at breakneck speed:
she was a bunch of dry vine shoots aflame
inside an oven fed by driving wind:
"Come running all and weep along with me,
poor folk, out from your lairs! He is now dead!
And he was murdered just to give you bread."

The mother took center stage in the poem alternating between expressions of tenderness and unbound love for her lost son and extreme violence to avenge his death, promising to tear the heart of the assassin from his chest with her bare hands. The mother-son relationship is one of the themes that is often visited by Buttitta in his long career. It is present in such poems as "The Convict's Return," "The Strike," "The Mothers of Children Miners," "A Mother's Lament," "The Mother's Milk," "The Crucifixion," "The Train of the Sun," "Purtedda dâ Ginestra," "Black Stones," and "Love Sillabary" to name some of the most famous. There is something obsessive about it, very likely because Buttitta had a poor relationship with his own mother. In one of his early poems, published in *La trazzera*, he complained that he had never known a caress from his mother. When he was born, his mother who already had four other children, gave him to a wet-nurse to feed and raise, while keeping the female of the twins with her. His mother's rejection at birth marked his soul for when he was sixty years old he wrote the poem "The Mother's Milk" ("Lu latti di la matri") in which he bared his open wound:

My mother
never gave me of her milk.
I can say that
I was born an orphan.
I was fed by a wet-nurse…
I grew old
without knowing
how mothers kiss;
how they embrace their children,
and what they feel inside their bones:
I think of it and shake!
I grew old
without knowing to whom
I should give my filial love
that time drew out of the fire,
and beat it burning upon
the anvil of my heart.

In these poems, the attachment of the mothers to their sons is visceral. The Christological images return in "A Mother's Lament," in which a mother who lost her son in the massacre of the "Purdedda dâ Ginestra" recalls delicate moments of tenderness and the agony of confronting her son's demise:

Quannu turnavi fincevi alligrizza,
ma nni la facci mustravi stanchizza;
iu ti stujava la frunti sudata
e tu mi davi la prima vasata,
ed iu: "mancia," e tu: "mancia cu mia,"
e s'assittava Gesu cu Maria:
Ahi! Ahi!

Ma ora nun ti sonnu mperaturi,
né cavaleri e mancu zappaturi,
si ti sunnassi jsassi li vuci
ca sì chiantatu comu Cristu ncruci.
Ahi! Ahi!

When you returned at night you feigned good cheer
but in your face your tiredness was clear.
I would then wipe the sweat off your forehead
and you repaid me with your first kiss
and I'd say "eat!" and "eat with me!' you'd say,
and Jesus sat with Mary every day.
Oh the sorrow!

But now I don't dream of you as a knight,
not a sod-buster nor an emperor.
If I should dream of you, I'd scream in horror
for I see you as Christ nailed to the cross.
Oh the sorrow!

The visceral attachment that mothers show for their sons in all these poems may be seen as conforming to the Mother-Son archetypal relationship, but may have been an unconscious desire to compensate for the lack of motherly love from his own mother. But while the mother-son relationship had definite autobiographical connections, it was part of Buttitta's approach to poetry. He was primarily interested in communicating with his listeners. I say listeners because Buttitta's poetry was meant to be spoken and not read silently. It was meant to be experienced from the voice of the author in a public square. This required that his words be readily understood by the people listening, his metaphors could not be abstruse, requiring reflection. They were meant to be perceived immediately from the living voice of the poet. The mother grieving for her murdered son is one of the most poignant images in Western Art. Michelangelo alone sculpted four different interpretations of the theme, the most famous being the "Pietà" that greets you from the first chapel on the right on entering St. Peter's in Rome. But in Sicily the image is pervasive at all levels. Out of the many possible events in the Madonna's life, the most common is that of the grieving mother. Indeed, Angelo Costanzo in an article published in *Arba Sicula* wrote that Sicilian women, as they go through the vicissitudes of life, slowly adopt on an unconscious level the image of the *mater dolorosa* (the Sorrowful Mother) as their own. Along the same lines, it is not surprising that the images of Christ that pervade the Sicilian psyche are restricted typically to those of the suffering Christ on the cross and Christ as a child, that is, suffering and innocence, an innocent victim slaughtered by powerful enemies in which one can see, by extension, the suffering of the poor people of Sicily at the hands of external and internal forces. In the "Lament for the Death of Turiddu Carnivali," Turiddu summoned the same image: "A Cristu l'ammazzaru e fu innuccenti," (They murdered Christ and he was innocent.) And Buttitta wrote of much suffering and innocence among the Sicilian people, whether he was singing of the lack of employment that caused one quarter of the Sicilian population to leave their home to find work in the coal mines of Belgium, as we read in his poem "Lu trenu di lu suli" and "L'emigranti ripartunu" or in the mines of West Virginia, or on the cotton plantations of Louisiana, where they would be exploited, insulted, called *terroni*, wops, dagoes; or the greed of landowners who exploited the laborers and farm workers by not paying them enough to buy a piece of bread for their families, as we saw in the poem "The Strike," in "Lament for Turiddu Carnivali" and in "Sicily Has a Master"; or the insanity of war that destroys so many lives on the battlefields and at home, as we saw in "Letter to a German Mother" and "A Century of History"; or the suffering of the *carusi*, young boys who were sold as slaves to work in the dreadful sulfur mines of Sicily whose plight is dramatically portrayed in the poem "A li matri di li carusi" ("To the Mothers of Children Sulfur Miners"); suffering and innocence is dramatically displayed in the massacre at the "Purtedda dâ Ginestra" where Giuliano's gang machine gunned a crowd celebrating Labor Day. In all these poems, Buttitta is on the side of the have nots, the poor, the hungry, and the oppressed. He denounces, condemns, and shames the powerful, the rich, the fascists and sometimes even the poor and the oppressed for not standing up, for their submissive nature and resignation, as in the poem "Parru cu tia" (I am Talking to You). Buttitta was a militant poet who went into the squares to recite his poems to large crowds of workers, urging them to unite, to fight for their rights as human beings, to join the struggle for equality and giving dignity to those who work. He stirred the crowd and was himself stirred by the crowd.

Buttitta's opus is replete with archetypal images that he adapts to express the concerns of his inner world. They are the universal values that every person yearns for in life, not connected exclusively with the local population of Bagheria or the entire island of Sicily. While condemning the injustices suffered by the Sicilian poor he is talking about the poor people of the earth, in denouncing the greed of the wealthy and their exploitation of the laborers, the farm hands, those who shed blood and sweat hoeing the land of owners who live in the cities, he is denouncing the system that allows such oppression to exist.

But Buttitta was not just a fierce street poet who could stir crowds and inflame their hearts. He was also a man who loved his fellow man and who believed that the oppressed, the weak one day would have the upper hand against the oppressors. He devoted his whole life to the ideal of equality and justice for all men. His was a Christian struggle. In the poem "Parru cu tia" in the last stanza he urged the oppressed to:

> Tear off that ragged, patched up shirt you wear,
> color it and transform it into a banner,
> red like the robe that Jesus Christ then wore,
> and let your arm and wrist be like a torch,
> make it wave in the wind like a tight fist
> red, all red, like the tunic worn by Christ!

And he never gave up his belief that some day man would find a more equitable way to live. He believed in Christ, not as the divine son of God, but as "the greatest poet, the greatest philosopher of all time," as he said once to Carlo Puleo. And Jesus Christ is the supreme embodiment of suffering and innocence as the poet portrays him in his "'Ncuntravu 'u Signuri," ("I Encountered the Lord") a remarkable poem in which his intense religious Christian feelings are expressed. The figure of Christ is placed at the center of the poet's spiritual longing, as Salvatore Di Marco, who has written extensively on Buttitta's poetry, pointed out. Buttitta's portrait of Jesus who walks barefoot with his bones gnawed by worms, a parched mouth, looking for water to drink, is a powerful metaphor of the suffering of the have nots. The last quartet of the poem recalls the injustice that is inherent in the concepts of suffering and innocence:

Era stancu,	He was exhausted,
mi taliava e chiancìa	he looked at me and he kept crying
comu unu nnuccenti	like an innocent man
ch'acchiana o patibulu.	climbing onto the gallows.

In this poem, as well as in the equally famous "The Crucifixion," the figure of Christ is portrayed as the embodiment of the concept of brotherly love among human beings, of sincere Christian solidarity that is perfectly in tune with the evangelical spirit. The initial quartet of the poem expresses the awe the poet felt before Christ's evangelical mission to change the destiny of man:

Non ci fu nuddu nta terra	No one on earth had ever
chi parrò comu iddu;	spoken the way he did;
nuddu chi sappi diri paroli	no one who knew how to convey
e nsignamenti	the words and the teachings
pi canciari u distinu di l'omu.	to change the destiny of man.

Even though Buttitta had espoused early in his career a socialist ideology he never allowed his political beliefs to taint his stronger belief in a humanism that has a religious quality to it. He differentiated between the official Catholicism and Christianity. In an interview with Franco Capelvenere, quoted by Marco Scalabrino in his *Ignazio Buttitta: dalla piazza all'universo* (p. 167) Buttitta said: "In all of us there is goodness and there is evil, and we men must defeat evil with love." The interviewer, who knew the poet's ideological convictions, objected that that was a Catholic concept, and Buttitta simply replied, "No, it is a Christian concept."

The poet wanted to be remembered for his love of humanity. In another interview with Maria Sciavarello he said that he wanted the following inscription to be placed on his tombstone: "Un poeta che amò il popolo." (A poet who loved people) (Scalabrino, p. 171).

He never changed his political beliefs, even though they were tested. One such moment came after a disconcerting conversation in Moscow with a woman whose husband, a doctor and a communist, had been killed by the Stalinists, Buttitta's faith in Russian socialism was deeply shaken. But he did not give up his dream to see better conditions for humanity. In the prologue to his "Pueta nta chiazza," a sort of testament to his life-long dream of redemption for the poor, he wrote in Italian:

Io credo nel socialismo,
credo nel tempo lungo
e lascio la vita cantando;
e voglio che chi mi conosce
possa dire: "Fu contadino e medico Ignazio,
strappava spine e piantava rose,
tagliava il male e sanava ferite."
Possa dire: "Fu poeta e marinaio,

navigava in acque inquinate
ma nel suo pezzo di mare
pescava pesci vivi."
Io credo nel socialismo:
so che il raccolto è lontano,
i frutti acerbi agli alberi,
e gli uomini hanno braccia corte
e piedi di piombo.
Ci credo,
e vedo l'alba di domani
con le braccia aperte sulla terra;
e se mi strappo gli occhi e ve li do
(così come sono,
pieni di luce e di fuoco),
la vedrete anche voi. *Aspra, marzo 1974*

I believe in Socialism
I believe in the long time
and I leave life singing;
and I want those who know me
to be able to say:
"Ignazio was a peasant and a physician,
who removed thorns and planted roses,
he cut away evil and healed wounds,"
To be able to say: "He was a poet and a sailor,
he sailed in polluted waters,
but in his portion of the sea,
he caught living fish."
I believe in socialism:
I know the harvest is far away
and fruits are not ripe on the trees,
and men have short arms
and feet made of lead.
I believe in it:
and I can see tomorrow's dawn.
with my arms open on the earth;
and if I tear my eyes out and give them to you
(just as they are,
full of light and fire),
you will see it too. *Aspra, March 1974*

Lu sciopiru

(Da *Sintimintali*)

I.
S'avanza la fudda - s'avanza purtannu
li coppuli 'mmanu - jsannu li vuci;
cc'è un vecchiu aggubbatu - ca pari me' nannu,
e porta a bannera - a modu di cruci.
Su' vecchi arrappati - su' donni patuti,
picciotti 'i campagna - chi nervi d'azzaru,
su' nichi sfardati - chi facci 'ngialluti,
su' milli... du' mila ... - Ma d'unni spuntaru?
-S'avanza la fudda: - Vulemu travagghiu!
Rispunni 'na vuci: - Mittiti 'nsirragghiu.

II.
La massa s'arresta ... - si movi, camina ...
allenta lu passu ... - ripigghia di bottu ...
si ferma 'n'anticchia ... - fà comu la china ...
avanza la fudda - currennu di trottu ...
un corpu ... du corpa ... - na scarrica 'ntera
la genti si sparti... - cu grida, cu chiama
chiancennu la matri - cu fujri spera,
cu cadi firutu: - succedi la strama ....

III.
'Na vecchia, mischina, - ch'aveva scuppatu
firuta a lu pettu - fà sforzi... si susi,
s'appoja a lu muru - du bustu 'nsangatu
lu sangu ci scula: - ci su' du' pirtusi.
Allonga lu pedi - vurrissi scappari,
la forza cci manca - lu sangu a li vini,
cci trema la gamma - nun pò caminari,
e cadi gridannu - tri voti: - Assassini!!

IV.
Ma eccu ca spunta - trimannu un surdatu,
cu ll'occhi 'nfucati - chi mannanu fiamma,

The Strike

1
The crowd's advancing, moving with their hats
held in their hands. Their voices growing loud.
There is an old man who is bent who looks
just like my grandpa, carrying a flag
that looks more like a cross. They're wrinkled, old,
they're women grieving, and young men from the fields,
with nerves of steel; they're children with gaunt faces:
One thousand, two... – where did they all come from?
The crowd is moving now – "We just want work!"
A voice was heard – Just throw them all in jail.

2
The crowd now stops – it starts again, it walks.
Then slows its pace, then suddenly it starts.
It pauses for a while – Then like a flood,
it moves, advancing, running at a trot.
One shot, then two...then shots that strafe at will.
The people start dispersing, some now scream,
while others cry, some call their mother's name,
some flee, some, wounded, fall like autumn leaves.

3
A poor old woman, who had fallen down,
is wounded in her chest. She struggles to get up,
she leans on the wall, blood is pouring out
from her bloodied chest. She has two holes there.
She then extends one foot trying to escape,
but has no strength, no blood inside her veins.
Her legs are shaking and she cannot walk.
She falls and screams "You, murderers!" Three times.

4
A soldier then comes, shaking visibly.
His eyes are red, they seem to be on fire,

è unu di chiddi - ch'aveva sparatu:
sò matri è la vecchia ... - la morta è sò mamma.
L'afferra... la spinci - l'abbrazza chiancennu ....
Ssrincennu li denti - com'arma addannata,
dicennuci: matri ! ? - Matruzza, cunprennu
lu mali chi fici, - pi l'arma du tata,
tu giuru ... sparai ... - sparai pi sbagghiu ...
'Na vuci cchiù forti: -- Arreri 'nsirragghiu ...

V.
- Avanti, sparati - ch'è chista a me' morti,
la morti cchiù santa - lu stessu distinu
pi mmatri e pi ffigghiu ... - tirati cchiù forti,
'mmazzai la matri... - cci· moru vicinu ! ...
un corpu ... du corpa: mischinu, ed abbucca
di 'ncoddu a sò matri ... - La chiama ... s'attacca
chiancennu o sò pettu ... - Ci vasa la vucca...
la frunti ... li manu ... - Ma prima ch'assacca,
c'u' filu di vuci - ch'è comu lu ciatu.
Ci dici: - Matruzza! ... - Scuttavi 'u piccatu ...

He's one of those who fired on the crowd.
The woman was his mother: mom's now dead.
He holds her, raises her, hugs her in tears.
Grinding his teeth, like one who's damned to hell,
He says, sweet Mother, Mother I'm aware
of the great harm I've wrought. I swear
on father's soul, I shot you by mistake.
A stronger voice was heard, imprison them!

5

Go on and shoot. This death is mine to own:
The holiest of deaths - same destiny,
a mother and her son… go on, shoot straight!
I killed my mother… let me die with her!
Behold two bodies: the poor wretch just flops
over his mother, calling, grasping her,
weeping on her. He kisses then her mouth,
her hands, her forehead, and before he dies,
he whispers with a voice that's like a sigh,
sweet Mother, I atone with my demise...

Sariddu lu Bassanu

(Da *La peddi nova*)

Sariddu lu Bassanu
fascista e talianu
è paisanu miu,
e mi nni vantu,
viva Diu!

Partìu pi la Spagna
e turnau cu na lasagna
longa di midagghi
a tanti tagghi
e lucenti, spirlucenti
comu fussiru pinnenti
nni lu pettu d'una fata:
un eroi, milli eroi,
una nuvula di eroi;
tirrimotu a li nnimici,
vampi, focu, morti e pici.
Sariddu lu Bassanu,
salutu rumanu.

Si mi passa pi davanti
lu me cori è trabballanti
ca mi pari sta figura
tutta china di lustrura;
un eroi di sta manera
luci comu na bannera;
ci vasassi lu vastuni
ci cadissi addinucchiuni,
ci allisciassi la firita
cu lu meli e cu la sita.
Quantu onuri p'un paisi
sti dui vrazza e gammi tisi
e lu pettu fraggillatu
comu Diu sacramintatu.
Sariddu lu Bassanu,
salutu rumanu.

Sariddu, the Highboot

Sariddu, the Highboot,
to whom I pay tribute
is a fascist and Italian,
and my own countryman
praise to the Lord!

He went to Spain one day
and when he came back home
he brought a honeycomb
of medals of all sizes
and wore those shiny prizes
as gems a fairy queen
wears part of her routine.
a hero, many heroes,
of heroes a big batch:
a terror to his foes:
flames, fire, death and pitch.
Sariddu, the Highboot,
Roman salute.
If he crosses in my wake
my heart then begins to shake,
for his figure seems to glow
like a banner at a show,
for a hero of this kind
is most difficult to find.
I would gladly kiss his cane,
on my knees I would remain,
I would stroke his injury
with silk, honey tenderly.
Oh the honor and renown
those stiff limbs gave to this town,
and that chest of his so gored
like the scourging of the Lord.
Sariddu, the Highboot,
Roman salute.

La so vita si fu lorda
ora nuddu la ricorda;
travagghiari un vosi mai:
jocu, vinu, liti e guai;
e la sira li so figghi
comu fussiru cunigghi
si mittevanu a la gnuni
cu li testi a pinnuluni,
e, diuni, li nuccenti
cu la fami nta li denti.
Sariddu lu Bassanu,
Salutu rumanu.

Una notti so muggheri
vitti suli, stiddi e sferi:
era junta a ddu mumentu
di aviri un nascimentu,
e Sariddu nta la panza
ci ballò na contralanza,
vuciannu: "Gran buttana,
sparagnamu la mammana";
e pistava la racina
cu na rabbia canina:
puviredda, ristò tisa
tra lu sangu e la cammisa.
Sariddu lu Bassanu,
salutu rumanu.

Quannu vinni a lu paisi
quantu ciuri, quantu spisi!
Primu a tutti lu prifettu
chi tinìa lu gagliardettu;
li fascisti alliniati,
alalà! tutti priati;
so muggheri, mmenzu a chiddi,
si strincìa li picciriddi,
spavintata, stanturuta,

If his life was base, morose,
now nobody really knows;
work was not a thing he chose:
just wine, gambling, fights and woes;
and his children when night came
with heads hanging down in shame,
in a corner went to hide
like scared rabbits, mortified.
Without food and without blame,
each night played the hunger game.
Sariddu, the Highboot,
Roman salute.

And one night his wretched wife
saw the sun, the stars, and strife.
As her labor pains commenced
and her hurting grew intense,
cool Sariddu with his hands
on her belly pressed and danced.
"Rotten whore!" he screamed aloud,
we've no need of a midwife."
And kept pressing out that life
with great anger like a hound.
The poor woman stiff, unsound,
in her night shirt soaked with blood,
was left weakened by that flood.
Sariddu, the Highboot,
Roman salute.

When to town he did come back,
many flowers, great expense!
Our prefect, first of the pack,
with the pennant in his hands.
Then the fascists all aligned
Alalà!, yelled with one mind.
His poor wife, now terrified,
clasped her kids close to her side.

ca pareva una spirduta;
ma la matri, la gna Cicca,
cu la facci virdi e sicca
e la vucca sgangulata
si faceva una risata,
arraspannusi la testa
comu fossi nta na festa;
e lu patri, a gran consigghiu,
nta dda fudda pi so figghiu
si sintìa lu cori chinu
e inniggiava a Mussulinu,
cu li vavi nta lu mussu
mbriacatu comu un ursu.
Sariddu lu Bassanu,
salutu rumanu.

Ci nn'è tanti a stu mumentu
di sti eroi di purtentu,
a riatta a cui cchiù sbrana
a cui tagghia carni umana;
li midagghi su a misura
di la morti e la svintura,
e cuntenti li paisi
si nni cantanu li mprisi;
ed iu cantu ad avuta vuci
a cui fici tanti cruci,
a Sariddu lu Bassanu
lu me beddu paisanu.
Sariddu lu Bassanu,
salutu rumanu.

In that crowd, she seemed to be
a poor soul adrift at sea.
But his mother, neighbor Fran,
with a face quite jaundiced, wan,
and her toothless mouth so wide,
laughed aloud to show her pride,
with one hand she stroked her hair,
like she was down at the Fair.
Having seen those hangers-on
who were there to praise his son,
his proud father then joined in,
and heaped praise on Mussolin,
while foam dribbled from his mouth
'cause he was drunk as a coot.
Sariddu, the Highboot,
Roman salute.

Many heroes do we see
all parading pompously,
who compete to tear apart
human beings with their art.
All their medals are a gage,
of the troubles of our age.
And our village is content
to applaud these foul events.
I deplore those who create
graveyard crosses with their hate.
To Sariddu the Highboot,
to my brave compatriot,
Sariddu the Highboot,
Roman salute.

La peddi nova

A Pier Paolo Pasolini

Certu era bellu scriviri
comu un briacu
a la taverna a bìviri,
chi guarda la buttigghia
e ci parra,
e ridi a lu bicchieri
chi svacanta
e torna a ghinchiri arreri.

Scriviri mprinatu d'amuri:
la gravidanza, li dogghi, lu partu,
lu tempu esattu
pi fari un figghiu
e nasciti na puisia.

Certu era bellu;
ma ora sugnu spirtusatu,
lazzariatu di dintra,
e scrivu
cu lu duluri chi mi torci
comu un sarmentu a lu furnu;
com'unu assicutatu di li spirdi
muzzicatu di li lapi.

La storia di st'anni fucusi
ha zappatu cu l'ugna
dintra di mia,
e restu scantatu a taliari
l'omini tutti
mpinnuliati a un filu,
a un distinu sulu,
dintra na varca di pagghia c'affunna.

The New Skin

To Pier Paolo Pasolini

Sure, it was beautiful to write
like a drunkard
inside a tavern drinking,
looking at the bottle
speaking to it,
laughing at the glass
that he is emptying
and filling it up again.

Writing, filled with love,
pregnancy, labors, birth,
the exact time
for giving birth
to a song and a poem.

Sure, it was beautiful;
but now I'm full of holes,
torn apart inside,
and I write
while pain's tormenting me
like a dry vine twig that burns,
like someone chased by ghosts
and stung by wasps.

The history of these fierce years
has dug its nails
inside of me,
and I'm left terrified to look
at all the men
hanging on a line,
on the same destiny,
in a straw boat that's foundering.

Sentu ca la me vuci
chi li chiama di luntanu
avi limmiti e cunfìni d'amuri
e mòri nni l'aria.
Vogghʼessiri un cocciu di rina
nni la rina di la praja;
un pisci nni la riti cu l'àutri
mpignati a sfunnari
la gaggia chi li chiuj.

Mi vogghiu svacantari, scurdari,
farimi la peddi nova
comu li scursuna.

I feel that my voice
that calls them from far away
has limitations and barriers of love
and fades in the air.
I want to be a grain of sand
in the sand of the beach;
a fish caught in the net with all the others
struggling to breach
the cage that holds them.

I want to empty myself, forget,
grow myself a new skin
like the snakes.

Li vuci di l'omini

(Da *La peddi nova*)
A Leonida Répaci

Quantu strati e paisi
e citati canusciu
e quantu treni
a scinniri ed acchianari;
quantu facci d'omini
di fimmini
di picciriddi chi salutanu,
e lu trenu chi passa
e li robbi stinnuti
e li trizzi di l'agghia a la finestra.

Quantu strata
cu li pedi chi dòlinu,
quantu mpinciuti
supra sidili di petra
cu l'ammogghiu vicinu
e li carusi
ca passanu a taliari
pi capiri cu sugnu.

Quantu notti e quantu voti
cuntari li picciuli
cu la manu
nni la sacchetta affunnata,
e l'umbri di l'omini
e li porti nzirrati
e lu cori chi squagghia comu cira.

Quantu notti e quantu voti
dumannari un lettu,
projri li carti
e ddà na fimmina grassa ca fuma
cu li gammi a cavaddu
e mi ridi·

The Voices of Men

To Leonida Répaci

How many streets, villages
and cities I have known
and how many trains
I've gotten on and off;
how many faces of men,
of women
of children waving goodbye,
while the train goes by
and clothes drying on a line
and garlic braids hanging in the windows.

How much walking
with throbbing feet,
how many stops to rest
on benches made of stone
with my bundle next to me
while passing children
stare at me
to understand who I am.

How many nights and how many times,
sinking my hand in my pocket
to count my money
what money remains,
and the shadows of men
behind locked doors
and my heart melting like wax.

How many nights and how many times
asking for a bed,
handing over papers
to a fat woman who is smoking
with her legs crossed
laughing a me,

arrunchiannu lu coddu;
e poi la càmmara scura,
lu tanfu di nchiusu,
lu lettu c'havi un patruni ogni sira
e li linzola ca fètinu
di carni stricati.

Quantu fumu nni sti càmmari,
cu li pinzeri orbi
ca truzzanu a li mura
e restanu mpinnuliati a lu tettu.

Quantu fumu;
ed iu a vasarimi li manu,
ad abbrazzarimi
pi sintirimi strinciri,
a chiamarimi: Gnaziu, Gnaziu,
pi nun essiri sulu.

Quantu fumu,
e lu cori assuppatu
comu muddica di pani vagnata.

Quantu notti
cu l'occhi cusuti e scusuti
e lu sonnu c'arriva a marusi
cu la forza d'un tàvaru.

Quantu notti e quantu fumu;
e poi l'arba
li primi fila di luci
lu ventu c'arrimina lu purtali
lu cantu di l'aceddi,
li vuci di l'omini.

Ed iu mi susu
cu li vuci di l' omini.

sinking inside her neck;
and then the dark room,
the stench of stagnant air,
the bed that changes owner every night
and the bedsheets that smell
of rubbing flesh.

How much smoke in these rooms,
with blind thoughts
that crash against the walls
and stay there hanging on the ceiling.

How much smoke;
and I just kiss my hands,
and hug myself
to feel somebody's touch
calling myself by name, Gnaziu, Gnaziu,
not to be alone.

How much smoke,
and the heart soaked
like the soft part of the bread in water.

How many nights
with my eyes sewn shut and unsewn
and sleep that arrives like breakers
with the power of a bull.

How many nights and how much smoke;
then dawn breaks
the first glimmers of light
the breeze that moves the curtains
the singing of birds
the voices of men.

And I get up
with the voices of men.

Li morti

(Da *La peddi nova*)

Li morti quannu mòrinu
nun mòrinu allura,
comu li serpi pistati
ca mòvinu la cuda
doppu morti,
comu li pisci piscati
ca sàtanu
nni lu funnu di la varca
e ciatanu ancora.

Nun mòrinu allura,
nun parranu;
ma seguitanu a campari,
e sunnu tisi, friddi, morti,
cu lu cori fermu.

Mòrinu doppu
a lu campusantu;
ma dintra
mentri li vestinu cu li robbi novi
e li conzanu nni lu catalettu
sunnu vivi,
e a chiddu chi ci torci li vrazza
pi nfilaricci la cammisa,
ci vurrissiru diri:
adaciu, nun mi struppiari.

E a la muggheri
(si sannu ca finci)
nun chianciri,
ci vurrissiru diri,
m'addisiavi la morti:
stanotti
nun mi senti tussiri

The Dead

When the dead die
they do not die then,
like snakes who move their tails
after being crushed
though they are dead,
like the caught fish
that jump
on the bottom of the boat
still breathing.

They don't die then,
they don't talk,
but they continue living,
and they are stiff, cold, dead,
with their hearts stopped.

They die later
at the cemetery;
but in the house
while being dressed in their new clothes
and laid on their deathbed
they are alive,
and to the one who twists their arm
to put the shirt on them
they feel like saying:
careful, you're hurting me.

And to their wives
(if they know they're faking it)
don't cry,
they feel like saying,
you wished me dead:
tonight
you will not hear me coughing

e mancu runfuliari.
E a li figghi,
li vurrissiru chiamari
e strinciricci li testi cu li manu
comu si fa cu li muluna.

Sentinu e vidinu li morti;
e si nun hannu mai jutu a la missa,
li paroli in latinu
chi dicinu li parrini,
si li mettinu a memoria,
li ripetinu.

Sunnu cuntignusi, li morti;
vurrissiru
ca lu funirali
facissi strati scògniti
e nun passassi di li chiazza
pi nun ncuntrari
lu putiaru c'avanza.

Ma li vivi
nun li capiscinu li morti;
e quannu li calanu nni li fossi
cu li cordi a chiaccu,
nun s'addunanu
ca li morti si disperanu,
ca si torcinu dintra li casci
e vurrissiru nèsciri.

Nun lu sannu li vivi
ca scuperchianu li casci
e a l'additta
cu li manu isati
appuntiddanu li pedi
pi ghisari li balati,
e chi furrìanu a lu scuru

and not even snoring.
And for their children
they feel like calling them
and squeeze their heads in their hands
as people do with melons.

The dead can hear and see;
and if they've never been to Mass,
they try to memorize
the Latin words
the priests recite,
repeating them.

The dead are reserved;
they would prefer
that the funeral procession
go through less common streets
avoiding the town's square
not to cross paths with the shopkeeper
to whom they owe money.

But living people
don't understand the dead;
and when they lower them inside their graves
with the rope that's like a noose,
they do not realize
that the dead are desperate,
that they are struggling inside their coffins,
wanting to get out.

Living people do not know
the dead push up
with their raised hands
to remove the lid of the casket
and that they stand up on their toes
to lift the tombstone,
and that they try to find a hole

pi truvari un pirtusu.

Nun lu sannu, li vivi,
ca li morti, sulu tannu,
misuranu la crudiltà di la vita.

searching in the dark.

Living people do not know
that only then the dead
can measure the cruelty of life.

Lu tempu e la storia

(Da *La peddi nova*)
A Carlo Levi

Quantu strata,
quantu lacrimi
e quantu sangu ancora, cumpagnu.

La storia zappa a cintimitru
e l'omini hannu li pedi di chiummu.
Nun parra l'amarizza
chi mi cummogghia lu cori stanotti,
né lu scuru supra li muntagni,
ma lu silenziu
di seculi luntani.

È la puisia
chi tocca lu pusu di la storia:
la vuci risuscitata di Maiakovski,
lu chiantu di Hiroshima,
lu lamentu di Garcia Lorca
fucilatu a lu muru.

Quannu ti pari c'arrivi,
si a l'accuminzagghia, cumpagnu;
nun t'avviliri di chissu,
seguita a svacantari
puzzi di duluri,
àvutri vrazza
doppu di tia e di mia virrannu.

A l'ingiustizia c'ammunzedda negghi
e nverni friddi
supra li carni di la terra,
ciusciacci lu focu di lu to amuri.

Nun ti stancari di scippari spini,
di siminari a l'acqua e a lu ventu;

Time and History

To Carlo Levi

What a long journey,
how many tears
how much more blood, comrade.

History hoes in inches
and men have feet of led.
What speaks in me tonight
is not the bitterness that covers my heart,
nor the darkness over the mountains,
but the silence
of distant centuries.

Poetry is
what touches the pulse of history:
Maiakovski's resurrected voice,
the weeping of Hiroshima
Garcia Lorca's lament,
shot against a wall.

When you think you have arrived,
you're just at the beginning, comrade;
Don't lose courage for this,
continue to empty out
wells filled with pain,
other arms
will come after you and me.

Blow the fire of your love
on the injustice that accumulates fogs
and frigid winters
upon the flesh of earth.

Don't tire of removing thorns,
of sowing in the rain and wind:

la storia nun meti a giugnu,
nun vinnigna a ottuviru,
havi na sula staciuni:
lu tempu.
Nun t'avviliri, cumpagnu,
si nun ti sacciu diri
quannu lu suli
finisci di siccari
li chiai di la terra.

history does not harvest in June
or in October.
It only has one season:
time.
Be not discouraged, comrade,
if I can't tell you
when the sun
will finish drying
the open wounds of earth.

Li pueti d'oggi

(Da *La peddi nova*)
A Cesare Zavattini

Pueta mpignatu
mi dicinu p'offisa;
comu si nun avissi la cammisa
e li robbi di ncoddu
e li scarpi a li pedi.
Comu s'un manciassi pani
pi stari all'additta
e nun mi stinnicchiassi a dòrmiri
cu la panza china, la notti.
Pecura senza lana
e sceccu senza cuda
mi vurrissiru:
n'abortu di natura.
Ca tali sunnu li pueti d'oggi,
aceddi senza gorgia,
aceddi orbi cu l'ali spinnati:
hannu lu munnu a mètiri
ed arricioppanu spichi
ntra lu pettu vacanti.
Schetti in viduvanza sunnu;
sunatura stunati
ca cercanu l'accordu
supra un filu di chitarra.
E nun sannu
ca lu pueta è marinaru
chi pisca cu lu tartaruni,
ca è aciddaru
cu li riti cunzati
tutti li staciuni.
E nun s'addunanu
ca la puisia
havi li radichi ntra la terra
e li rami ciuruti

Today's Poets

To Cesare Zavattini

They call me an engaged poet
as an insult;
as though I wore no shirts
and clothes on my body
and shoes on my feet.
As though I don't eat bread
to stand upright
and do not lay in bed at night
to sleep with a full stomach.
They would like me to be
a sheep without wool
a donkey with no tail:
a freak of nature.
For that's what today's poets are,
birds without a throat,
blind birds with featherless wings.
They have the world to harvest
and they survey
their empty breasts.
Unmarried men who mourn dead wives;
tone deaf musicians
seeking to tune a guitar string.
And they don't realize
that a poet is a sailor
who fishes with a fine net,
that he is a bird hunter
with nets that are in place
in every season.
And they don't realize
that poetry
has roots deep in the earth
and flowering branches
that like a man's arms

aperti ali' aria
comu vrazza d'omu.
Pueti senza mpegnu, vi salutu;
cugghiti pruvulazzu!
"Sulità e santità"
sunnu li vostri paroli;
ma la virità,
oggi e sempri,
resta mmenzu all'omini.

are open to the air.
Poets who are not engaged,
I salute you:
gather dust!
“Loneliness and holiness”
are words you like;
but truth,
today and always,
remains among men.

Lu prestitu

(Da *La peddi nova*)

Vaiu nni me frati a prestitu
sidd'haiu bisognu picciuli,
ca iddu nn'havi a bizzeffi
e li duna a lu trenta pi centu.

Ci vaiu pi nun mòriri,
quann'haiu cambiali scaduti
e l'usceri chi mi cerca
cu li carti nmanu.

Ci vaiu pi cridiri c'haiu un frati,
ma senza spiranza d'aiutu;
ed acchianannu li scali
(p'addivintari bonu
ed attruvari li paroli)
mi mettu a ricurdari
quann'eramu nichi,
ca durmevamo nzemmula
e ghiavamu ncampagna
a nchiaccari serpi;
e penzu a ddu mumentu
c'havi la stissa vuci di mia,
li stissi gesti e forsi
nni lu sangu d'usuraiu
na stizza di puisia.

Iddu a lu tràsiri
mi capisci nta l'occhi:
"assèttati", mi dici
e mi proj a biviri
pi pigghiari tempu
e sturnari lu discursu
ca iu nun sacciu cuminciari.

The Loan

I go to see my brother
if I should need a loan,
he has money to burn
and lends at thirty percent.

I go there not to die
when bills are overdue
and bill collectors chase after me
with papers in their hands.

I go there to believe I have a brother,
but without hoping he would help;
and as I climb those stairs
(to become more amiable
and to find the right words)
I try to remember
when we were children,
sleeping in the same bed
and went to the countryside
to catch snakes with a noose;
and then I ponder that
he has the same voice I have,
the same gestures and perhaps
a little drop of poetry
inside his usurer's blood.

As soon as I go in
he looks into my eyes and knows:
"Sit down," he says to me
and offers me a drink
to play for time
and change the subject
that I don't know how to begin.

Acchianu pi nun mòriri
e mi nni scinnu catavaru;
dda scala mi pari un puzzu,
un puzzu funnutu
e fora, strangusciatu,
pi nun chianciri;
mi fermu a taliari ntra l'occhi
li picciriddi chi passanu.

I climb those stairs not to die
and I climb down a corpse.
Those stairs seem like a well,
a bottomless well,
and when, distraught, I go outside
not to begin to cry,
I pause and look at the eyes
of the children passing by.

A li matri di li carusi

(Da *La peddi nova*)

Matri,
chi mannati li figghi a la surfara,
iu vi dumannu
pirchì a li vostri figghi
ci faciti l'occhi
si nun ponnu vidiri lu jornu?
Pirchì ci faciti li pedi
si caminanu a grancicuni?

Nun li mannati a la surfara;
si pani un nn'aviti,
scippativi na minna,
un pezzu di mascidda
pi sazialli.

Disiddiraticci la morti cchiuttostu,
megghiu un mortu mmenzu la casa
stinnicchiatu supra un linzolu arripizzatu,
ca lu putiti chianciri
e staricci vicinu.

Megghiu un mortu cunzatu
supra lu lettu puvireddu
di la vostra casa
cu la genti chi veni a vidillu
e si leva la còppula
mentri trasi.

Megghiu un mortu dintra
ca vrudicatu sutta la surfara,
cu vuàtri supra dda terra a chianciri
a raspari cu l'ugna
a manciarivi li petri
a sentiri lu lamentu
e nun putiricci

To the Mothers of Children Miners

Mothers,
who send your children
to the sulfur mines, to you I say:
why did you make them eyes,
if they can't see the light of day?
Why did you make them feet
if they must crawl on all fours?

Don't send them to the sulfur mines!
If you do not have bread for them,
cut off one of your breasts,
a piece of your jaw
to satisfy their hunger.

Better to wish them dead instead;
better to have a dead boy in your home,
laid out upon a patched up sheet,
where you can weep for him,
and then remain close by his side.

Better to have a dead boy all laid out
upon a poor man's bed
in your own house
where people who come to see him
take off their caps
when they come in.

Better to have a dead boy in your home
than buried in the sulfur mine
with you weeping
on the surface,
scratching the dirt
with your fingernails,
eating away the rocks,
listening to their lament,

livari di ncoddu
li petri chi lu scafazzanu.

Facitili di surfaru li figghi!

unable to remove the rocks,
that continue crushing them.

Make your children out of sulfur!

Lamentu di na matri
Nel giorno dell'eccidio di Portella della Ginestra

(Da *La peddi nova*)

Figghiu, quannu tu eri picciriddu,
satavi pi li strati comu un griddu;
un ghiornu mi purtasti na farfalla
cu l'ali d'oru e la tistuzza gialla:

Comu to patri fusti zappaturi
e ti susevi cu li primi arburi;
e fora di la porta, cu la manu,
mi salutavi ancora di luntanu:
Ahi! Ahi!
Ahi! Ahi!

Quannu turnavi fincevi alligrizza,
ma nni la facci mustravi stanchizza;
iu ti stujava la frunti sudata
e tu mi davi la prima vasata,
ed iu: "mancia," e tu: "mancia cu mia,"
e s'assittava Gesu cu Maria:
Ahi! Ahi!

Poi ca lu sonnu vineva mprisciatu
t'addummiscevi a lu vrazzu appujatu,
iu ti spugghiava adaciddu-adaciddu
e cu lu ciatu p'un sentiri friddu;
poi mi curcava cu tia vicinu,
cu la me testa nni lu to cuscinu:

Una nuttata mi sunnai ch'eri
addivintatu un granni cavaleri,
lu mperaturi di li paladini,
Ahi!

cu Orlannu e Rinardu malantrini,

A Mother's Lament
On the Day of the Massacre of Portella della Ginestra

My son, when you were just a little boy,
you jumped and ran just like a wound-up toy.
One day you brought me a small butterfly
with golden wings and with a yellow head.

Just like your father you were a sod-buster,
and you got up with the first sign of luster:
and then you waved goodbye out of the door
and turned around when far to wave once more.
Oh the sorrow!
Oh the sorrow!

When you returned at night you feigned good cheer
but in your face your tiredness was clear.
I would then wipe the sweat off your forehead
and you repaid me with your first kiss
and I'd say "eat!" and "eat with me!' you'd say,
and Jesus sat with Mary every day.
Oh the sorrow!

Then when your sleep came rushing over you,
you fell asleep by leaning on your arm,
and I undressed you slowly, very slowly
and with my breath I then would keep you warm.
Then I would lay down next to you, up close,
with my head resting on your pillowcase:

I dreamt that you one magic night
had just become a mighty knight,
Commander of the Paladins,
Oh the sorrow!

and with Orlando and Rinaldo, proud,

e tu trasevi cu banneri ntesta
ntra na citati e ti facìanu festa.
Curria la genti a fàriti rigali:
una jumenta gàvuta cu l'ali
un elmu ca pareva un campanaru
e na curazza d'oru ti purtaru:
Ahi!

Ma ora nun ti sonnu mperaturi,
né cavaleri e mancu zappaturi,
si ti sunnassi jsassi li vuci
ca si chiantatu comu Cristu ncruci.
Ahi! Ahi!

Ora nun parri, un vidi, un mi rispunni,
surdu comu la terra e comu l'unni;
ora nun parti e torni cu lu scuru
e l'occhi mei percianu lu muru:
Ahi! Ahi!

Ora un ti spogghiu, figghiu, un t'addummisciu,
si ncugnu a lu to lettu m'attirrisciu,
e si la testa appoju a lu cuscinu,
sbutta lu sangu, e viu lu lettu chinu:
Ahi! Ahi!

you marched with banner high in the first place.
The cheering in that city was so loud;
people ran to your side to give you gifts:
they brought you a tall mare with ample wings
a mighty shield that made you look so bold
and then a suit of armor made of gold.
Oh the sorrow!

But now I don't dream of you as a knight
not a sod-buster nor an emperor.
If I should dream of you, I'd scream in horror
for I see you as Christ nailed to the cross.
Oh the sorrow!

Now you don't speak, nor see or answer me.
You are deaf like the earth and waves at sea;
now you don't leave and don't come back at night,
and I pierce through the wall with my eyesight.
Oh the sorrow!

I don't undress you, son, or sing you lullabies.
If I approach your bed, I'm terrified,
if on your pillow I should rest my head,
blood overflows and saturates the bed.
Oh the sorrow!

Parru cu tia

(Da *Lu pani si chiama pani*)

Parru cu tia,
to è la curpa;
cu tia, mmenzu sta fudda
chi fai l'indiffirenti
tra na fumata e n'àutra di pipa
chi pari ciminera
sutta di sta pampera
di la coppula vecchia e cinnirusa.

Parru cu tia,
to è la curpa.
Guardatilu chi facci!
La purpa supra l'ossa un àvi tracci:
ci la sucau lu vermi di la fami;
e la mammana
ci addutau, ddu jornu
chi lu scippò di mmenzu a li muddami,
pani e cipudda.

Parru cu tia,
to è la curpa
si porti lu sidduni
e un ti lamenti;
si lu patruni, strincennu li denti,
cu lu marruggiu mmanu e la capizza
t'arrimodda li corna e ti l'aggrizza,
ti smancia li garruna,
ti fudda ntra li cianchi purpittuna,
t'ammacca ossa e spaddi,
ti sfricunia li caddi,
ti scorcia li crustani,
ti spurpa comu un cani,
e supra la to carogna

I Am Talking to You

I'm talking to you,
you are at fault;
to you, who stand there in the crowd,
feigning indifference
between each puff of smoke from your old pipe
that seems a chimney
under the peak
of your old and dusty cap.

I'm talking to you,
you are at fault.
Look at that face of his!
There is no trace of flesh upon his bones.
It was sucked out by hunger worms;
and the midwife
the day she pulled him
out of his mother's womb
she fated him to eat
onions with bread.

I'm talking to you,
you are at fault;
If you bear a pack saddle
and don't complain;
if your boss, grinding his teeth,
with a stick and a halter
softens your horns and makes them straight
wearing out your hocks,
landing blows on your sides
bruising your bones and shoulders,
skinning your callouses,
ripping the crusts off your sores,
grinding your flesh like dogs do bones

ci sputa e ti svirgogna.
Parru cu tia,
to è la curpa.
Ti dici lu parrinu:
"li beni di lu munnu
su fàusi
e murtali
ca ddà supra tutti scausi
arrivamu
e tutti aguali";
e tu ci cridi
e cali la tistazza
comu na pecura pazza,
e nun t'adduni
ca sutta lu rubbuni
c'è un utru pi panzuni
e la saurra
nfoca lu jocu di la murra;
e tu ci cridi e ti scordi
dda tana e ddu pirtusu
unni sdivachi l'ossa;
e li to figghi ntra dda fossa
cu li panzi vacanti
e li vrazzudda all'aria,
giarni comu malaria,
sicchi e sucati
com'umbri mpiccicati
a lu muru,
schelitri e peddi di tammuru;
ca si disianu farfalli
pi essiri vistuti,
agneddi pi sentiri cavudu
e gatti e cani pi spurpari ossa.

Parru cu tia,
to è la curpa
si la to casa pari un barraccuni

and spitting upon your carcass, humiliating you.
I'm talking to you,
you are at fault.
The priest says to you:
"The wealth of this world
is ephemeral
and mortal
because up there
we all arrive barefoot
and all equal;"
and you believe it
and lower your dumb head,
like a crazy sheep
and do not realize
that underneath that ample robe
he has a huge belly
like an inflated goat skin
and the dead wood
kindles the *morra* game;
and you believe it and forget
that lair, that hole
where you sink your bones
and in that hole your children
with empty stomachs
and their thin arms in air,
yellowed by malaria,
dried up and sucked up
like shadows stuck on the wall,
skeletons with skins for tambourines;
who wished to be butterflies
to be wearing clothes,
lambs to feel the warmth
and cats and dogs to chew on bones.

I am talking to you,
you are at fault;
if your house looks like a tent

di zingari sfardati:
la scupa ntra na gnuni
e scorci di patati,
lu cufularu cinniri,
di crita la pignata;
e to muggheri l'ossa
di pecura spurpata;
li matarazzi chini
di crinu di zabbara
e matri patri e figghi
tutti ntra na quadara;
lu sceccu, a vista d'occhi,
chi piscia e fa scumazza
gialla, ca la ristuccia
ntra li vudedda sguazza;
e fradicia, appizzata
a pignu nta l'arcova,
una cucuzza pàpara
ca premi russu d'ova;
e la fami chiantata
all'antu di la porta
cu li granfazzi aperti
e la vuccazza torta.

Sfarda sta cammisazza arripizzata,
tincila e fanni un pezzu di bannera,
trasi dintra li casi puvireddi,
scinni nni li carusi carzarati,
sduna pi li stratuna e li trazzeri,
chiama picciotti e vecchi jurnateri,
cerca dintra li funnachi e li grutti
l'omini persi, abbannunati e rutti,
gridacci cu la vuci d'un liuni:
"genti, vinni lu jornu a li diuni!"

Sfarda sta cammisazza arripizzata,
tincila e fanni un pezzu di bannera,

of rag-wearing gypsies:
the broom down in a corner,
and potato skins,
ashes in the hearth
pots made of clay;
and your wife with bones
like a fleshless sheep;
the mattresses full
of agave fibres
and mother, father, children
all in the same cauldron;
the donkey visible to all
who urinates creating
a yellow foam because
the stubble sloshes in its belly;
and hanging like
a pine cone on the alcove
a soft and rotting squash
drips red like egg yolk;
and hunger stuck
on the door jamb
with claws exposed
and with its ugly crooked mouth.

Tear off that ragged patched up shirt you wear,
color it and transform it into a banner,
enter the house of those who are dirt poor,
go down to where the children miners are
condemned, run through roadways and paths,
call out the young men and old laborers,
go search inside warehouses and in caves
for men who are forsaken, broken, lost,
shout to them with a lion's mighty voice:
"The time for hungry people has arrived!"

Tear off that ragged, patched up shirt you wear,
color it and transform it into a banner,

russa comu la tonaca di Cristu;
pi torcia lu to vrazzu e lu to pusu,
unniala a li venti a pugnu chiusu:
russa era la tonaca di Cristu! Russa!

red like the robe that Jesus Christ then wore
and let your arm and wrist be like a torch,
make it wave in the wind like a tight fist
red, all red, like the tunic worn by Christ!

Littra a na mamma tedesca

(Da *La peddi nova*)

Mamma tedesca,
quannu t'arriva sta littra
nni ddu paisi nicu e luntanu,
nta dda casa tirrana c'un ghiardineddu chiusu di sipali
e un cancellu di lignu:
mamma tedesca,
quannu t'arriva sta littra,
appizzala a lu ritrattu di to figghiu,
a lu capizzu di ddu lettu biancu
chi t'arristò vacanti.

Mamma tedesca,
ti scrivi ddu surdatu talianu
chi t'ammazzò lu figghiu.

Mmaliditta dda notti
e l'acqui di lu Piavi
e li cannuna e li bummi
e li luci chi c' eranu;
mmaliditti li stiddi
si lu manciassi a picca a picca:
un ghiditu, na manu,
un pedi, la facci;
e l'urtima palata,
e la terra chi crisci
chi crisci e fa la carni terra.

Nun c'eri,
mamma tedesca;
ma poi ti ntisi
chianciri e gridari
ntra dda càmmara,
sula,

A Letter to a German Mother

German mother,
when you receive this letter
in that small town so far away,
in that small house surrounded by a fence of cactus leaves
and a wooden gate;
German mother,
when you receive this letter,
pin it to the picture of your son
on the headboard of that white bed
that now lays empty.

German mother,
I'm the Italian soldier
who murdered your son.

Damn that night
and the waters of the Piave River
and the cannons and the bombs
and the lights that were there;
damn the stars
let earth consume him little at the time:
a finger, a hand,
a foot, his face;
and the last shovelful,
and the earth that grows
that grows and turns his flesh to earth.

But you weren't there,
German mother;
but then I heard you
crying and screaming
inside that room,
alone,

di ddu paisi luntanu;
ti vitti ittata
supra di ddu lettu
vacanti di to figghiu,
e fuddari la testa
sutta lu cuscinu,
e turciriti li manu,
e vuci e vuci,
comu si ntra lu pettu
scatinati
avissi centu armali
e milli vucchi pi lu to lamentu.

Sempre ti vitti e viu,
mamma tedesca,
vistuta di nivuru,
li vrazza all'aria,
e dintra l'occhi
lu figghiu mortu
cu li manu ncruci.

Sempre ti vitti
poi ca turnai
cu l'àvutri surdati
mmenzu fuddi di mammi filici,
quannu lu trenu firmava.

Sempre ti viu
si ntra la notti sentu,
tra muru e muru,
lu cantu di na matri.

Mamma tedesca,
iu, l'assassinu
ca ti livai lu figghiu:
comu pozzu dòrmiri
ed abbrazzari li me picciriddi?

from that far away country;
I saw you stretched
across the bed
that was your son's,
and sink your head
under his pillow
torturing your hands,
and scream, scream,
as though a hundred animals
and a hundred voices
had been unleashed
to utter your lament.

I always saw you and still do,
German mother,
dressed in black,
with arms up in the air,
and in your eyes
your dead son
with his hand crossed.

I always saw you
after I returned
with the other soldiers
surrounded by a crowd of happy mothers,
when the train stopped.

I always see you
if I hear during the night
between two walls
the singing of a mother.

German mother,
how can I sleep,
and hug my children,
I, the murderer,
who took your son from you?

Comu pozzu passari
mmenzu a l' omini boni
senz'essiri assicutatu,
e crucifissu a lu muru?

Tu ci jucavi mmenzu lu jardinu,
lu criscevi cu lu ciatu,
cu li suspira:
iu mi nzignava a sparari
comu megghiu putissi
ammazari a to figghiu.

Mamma tedesca,
matri di tuttu lu munnu,
vi chiamu!
Ognuna,
la petra cchiù grossa
vinissi a ghittalla.
supra di mia:
muntagni di petra,
muntagni di petra,
scacciati la guerra.

How can I walk
among good men
without being chased
and crucified upon a wall?

You played with him in your garden,
you raised him with your breath
with your sighs;
I was learning how to shoot,
how to best
murder your son.

German mother,
mothers of the whole world,
I call on you!
Let each of you
come hurl
the largest stone you find
upon my head:
mountains of stones,
mountains of stones,
chase away war.

Non sugnu pueta

(Da *Io faccio il poeta*)

Non pozzu chiànciri
haju l'occhi sicchi
e lu me cori
è comu un balatuni.

La vita m'arriddussi
asciuttu e mazziatu
comu na carrittata di pirciali.

Non sugnu pueta;
odiu lu rusignolu e li cicali,
lu venticeddu chi accarizza l'erbi
e li fogghi chi càdinu cu l'ali;
amu li furturati,
li venti chi strammìanu li negghi
ed annèttanu l'aria e lu celu.

Non sugnu pueta;
ma mancu un pisci greviu d'acqua duci;
sugnu un pisci mistinu
abituatu a li mari funnuti:
Non sugnu pueta
si puisia significa
la luna a pinnuluni
c'aggiarnìa li facci di li ziti;
a mia, la menzaluna,
mi piaci quannu luci
dintra lu biancu di l'occhi a lu voj.

Non sugnu pueta
ma siddu è puisia
affunnari li manu
ntra lu cori di l'omini patuti
pi spremiri lu chiantu e lu scunfortu;

I'm Not a Poet

I cannot weep
my eyes are dry
and my heart's like
a heavy tombstone.

Life has broken me
into a sterile load
of gravel for the road.

I'm not a poet
I hate warblers and cicadas,
little breezes kissing grass
and leaves that waft down to the ground.
I love great storms,
winds that overpower clouds
and clear the air and sky.

I am not a poet,
but not a bland fresh-water fish.
I am a marauding fish,
at home in the deep ocean.
I am not a poet
if by poetry you mean
the hanging crescent moon
that pales lovers' faces;
I'm one who likes the half moon
when it glistens in the whites
of a bull's eyes.

I am not a poet
but if by poetry you mean
sinking your hands inside
the hearts of men in pain
to squeeze out their despair and grief,

ma siddu è puisia
sciògghiri u chiaccu e nfurcati,
gràpiri l'occhi a l'orbi,
dari la ntisa e surdi,
rumpiri catini lazzi e gruppa:
(un mumentu ca scattu!)...

Ma siddu è puisia
chiamari ntra li tani e nta li grutti
cu mancia picca e vilena agghiutti;
chiamari li zappatura
aggubbati supra la terra
chi suca sangu e suduri;
e scippari
du funnu di surfari
la carni cristiana
chi coci nto nfernu:
(un mumentu ca scattu!)...

Ma siddu è puisia
vuliri milli
centumila fazzuletti bianchi
p'asciucari occhi abbuttati di chiantu;
vuliri letti moddi
e cuscina di sita
pi l'ossa sturtigghiati
di cu travagghia;
e vuliri la terra
un tappitu di pampini e di ciuri
p'arifriscari nta lu sò caminu
li pedi nudi di li puvireddi:
(un mumentu ca scattu!)

Ma siddu è puisia
farisi milli cori
e milli brazza
pir strinciri poviri matri

if by poetry you mean
undoing the noose of hanging men,
opening the eyes of men who cannot see,
making the deaf hear again,
breaking chains, bonds, and knots:
(wait a moment, I'm about to burst!)...

But if by poetry you mean
to call out to those who eat poorly,
swallowing poisons in their lairs and caves;
to call out sod-busters
bending over the earth
that sucks out blood and sweat;
and to tear away
the burning human flesh
from the hellish
sulfur mines:
(wait a moment, I'm about to burst!)...

But if by poetry you mean
wanting one-thousand,
one-hundred thousand white handkerchiefs
to dry the tears from swollen eyes,
wanting soft beds
and pillowcases made of silk
for the warped bones
of those who work;
and wanting earth to be
a carpet of flowers and of leaves
to cool the bare feet of the poor
walking in their journey:
(wait a moment, I'm about to burst!)

But if by poetry you mean
to sprout
a thousand hearts and arms
to hug poor mothers

assiccati du tempu e di la suffirenza
senza latti nta li minni
e cu u figghiu nta li brazza:
quattru ossa stritti
a lu pettu assitatu d'amuri:
(un mumentu ca scattu!)

datimi na vuci putenti
pirchì mi sentu pueta:
datimi nu stendardu di focu
e mi seguano li schiavi di la terra,
na ciumara di vuci e di canzuni:
li stracci all'aria
li stracci all'aria
assammarati di chiantu e di sangu...

withered by time and suffering
without milk in their breasts
with infants in their arms
who are just skin and bones
against a breast thirsting for love:
(wait a moment, I'm about to burst!)

then give me a powerful voice
because I feel I am a poet:
give me a banner of fire
and let the slaves of the earth follow me,
a flood of voices and of songs:
brandishing their rags
brandishing their rags
drenched with tears and blood...

Un seculu di storia

(Da *Io faccio il poeta*)

Accusu i politici
d'oggi e d'aeri:
Crispi e compagni,
pridicatura da monarchia,
beccamorti e fallignami
ca nchiuvaru a Sicilia
viva nta cruci.

Accusu i Savoia,
i primi e l'ultimu
re e imperaturi,
fascista e talianu
ncurunatu di midagghi
scippati cu sangu
nto cori di matri.

Un seculu di guerri,
un seculu di stragi:
c'è ossa di siciliani
vrudicati nte diserti,
nta nivi,
nto fangu di ciumi:
c'è sangu di sulfarara,
di zappatura,
di matri scheletri
e picciriddi sparati
nte chiazzi da Sicilia.

Non hannu vuci e gridanu
l'ammazzati du '93
chi petri nte sacchetti
e la fami nte panzi vacanti.

A Century of History

I accuse the politicians
of today and yesterday:
Crispi and his comrades
who preached monarchy,
gravediggers and carpenters
who nailed Sicily
on a cross alive.

I accuse the Savoy family,
the first and the last
king and emperor,
fascist and Italian
crowned with medals
torn out with blood
from the hearts of mothers.

A century of wars,
a century of massacres:
there are Italian bones
buried in deserts,
in snow,
in river mud:
there's blood of sulfur miners,
of sod-busters,
of mothers skin and bones
and children shot
in the squares of Sicily.

Those murdered in 1993
have no voices but they scream,
with rocks in their pockets
and hunger in their empty bellies.

Non hannu vuci e gridanu
cu coddu sutta i pedi di baruna,
cu l'ossa sturtiggnati du travagghiu;
ca lingua i cani
e u ciatu e denti.

Tri ghiorna di macellu
di martorii e beccamorti
di lamenti e chiantu
nte casi di poviri.

Ci fu carni a bon prezzu
nte tavuli di baruna;
a bon prezzu
pi sovrani di Roma;
a bon prezzu pi Crispi,
macillaru di corte;
e Lavriano
ginirali e sicariu
pagatu a ghiurnata.

L'avemu cca
ancora cca
chi stissi facci
e u cori di sarvaggi
i scannapopulu;
ci liccamu i pedi,
ci damu u votu,
l'ugnia pi scurciarinni;
a corda pi nfurcarinni;
a mazza e a ncunia
pi rumpirinni l'ossa.

L'avemu cca
ancora cca a mafia,
assittata nte vanchi d'imputati
a dittari liggi;

They have no voices and they scream
with their necks under barons' feet,
with their bones warped by work:
with tongues like dogs
and breathing heavily.

Three days of massacres
of mourning bells and gravediggers
of laments and tears
in the poor people's homes.

There was cheap meat
at the tables of the barons;
inexpensive
for the Roman sovereigns
inexpensive for Crispi,
the Court butcher;
and Lavriano,
general and assassin
paid by the day.

We have them here
still here
with the same faces
and hearts of savages
the people-butchers;
we lick their feet
we give them votes,
the nails to excoriate us,
the rope to hang us,
the hammer and the anvil,
to crush our bones.

We have them here
with the mafia still here,
sitting on defendants' benches,
dictating laws;

a scriviri sintenzi di morti
chi manu nsangati.

L'avemu cca
i compari da mafia
chi manu puliti,
i firrara di chiavi fausi,
i spogghia artari ca cruci nto pettu;
unni posanu i pedi sicca l'erba,
sicca l'acqua
spuntanu spini e lacrimi pa Sicilia.

L'avemu cca
l'affamati du putiri;
l'affamati di carni cruda,
ca cridinu a Sicilia
un porcu scannatu
e ci spurpanu l'ossa.

Si sì sicilianu
isa u vrazzu,
grapi a manu:
cincu banneri russi,
cincu!
Adduma a pruvulera du cori!

Si sì sicilianu
fatti a vuci cannuni,
u pettu carru armatu,
i gammi cavaddi di mari:
annea i nimici da Sicilia!

L'avemu cca e cantanu
i rusignoli ammaistrati
c'agghiuncinu lacrimi di nchiostru
e lacrimi da Sicilia,
e stornellanu u misereri

writing sentences of death
with bloody hands.

We have them here
the brothers of the mafia
with clean hands,
the smiths who make false keys
the altar thieves with crosses on their chests;
where they step the grass dies,
water dries out
and thorns sprout and tears for Sicily.

We have them here,
the ones who lust for power;
those hungry for raw meat
who think that Sicily
is a slaughtered pig
whose flesh they can consume.

If you're Sicilian
raise your arm,
open your hand;
five red banners,
five!
Kindle the powder keg inside your heart!

If you're Sicilian
make your voice a cannon,
your chest a tank,
your legs sea horses:
drown the enemies of Sicily!

We have them here, singing,
like trained nightingales
who add tears of ink
to the tears of Sicily.
And they sing the *miserere*

a gloria di patruna.
Cantanu odi o suli
o celu
o mari
a zagara,
e portanu a Sicilia ntronu
cu velu niuru
di mala maritata.

U furnu svampa
e ghettanu cinniri a palati,
incapaci d'impastari
i cori di siciliani
e farinni unu a tri punti
tridici voti chiù granni da Sicilia.

A Sicilia non havi chiù nomi
né casa e paisi;
havi i figghi sbattuti pu munnu
sputati comu cani,
vinnuti all'asta:
surdati disarmati
chi cummattinu chi vrazza.

Chi vrazza,
i rami virdi da Sicilia,
arrimiscanu a terra,
rumpinu timpuna,
siminanu
e fannu orti e ghiardina.

Chi vrazza,
fabbricanu palazzi,
costruiscinu scoli,
ponti,
officini
e aeroporti.

to the glory of the bosses.
They sing their hatred to the sun
to heaven
the sea
to orange blossoms,
and carry Sicily upon a throne
with a black veil
of one poorly wed.

An oven is blazing,
and they throw out shovelful of ashes,
unable to kneed
the heart of Sicilians
and create one with three points
thirteen times bigger than Sicily.

Sicily has no more names,
neither a home nor country;
its children thrown out to the world
spat out like dogs,
and sold at auction:
unarmed soldiers
who fight with their arms.

With their arms,
the green branches of Sicily
break up the sod,
break up the slopes,
and sow
creating orchard and groves.

With their arms...,
they raise buildings,
build schools,
bridges,
factories,
and airports.

Chi vrazza,
i lapi di meli da Sicilia
grapinu strati,
spirtusanu muntagni,
svacantanu a panza da terra.

Chi vrazza,
i surdati senza patria,
i sfardati,
i carni senza lardu
vestinu d'oru i porci di fora.
I chiamanu terroni,
zingari,
pedi fitusi;
e hanno i figghi e i matri
chi cuntanu i jorna
cu l'occhi vagnati;
e stu cielu ca vasu,
e sta terra chi toccu
e mi canta nte manu;
e seculi di civiltà
sutta i pedi.

A Sicilia non havi chiù nomi;
ma miliuna di surdi e di muti
affunnati nta un puzzu
ca io chiamu e non sentinu,
e s'allongu i vrazza
mi muzzicanu i manu.

Io ci calassi i cordi di vini,
i riti di l'occhi
pi tiralli du puzzu;
pirchì cca nascivu
e parru a lingua di me patri;
e i pisci
aceddi

With their arms,
the honeybees of Sicily
cut new roads,
tunnel through mountains,
empty out the bowels of the earth.

With their arms,
the soldiers with no motherland
worn-out,
with flesh that has no fat
dress foreign pigs with gold.
They call them dirt eaters,
gypsies,
stinky feet,
and they have sons and mothers
who count the days
with tears in their eyes;
and this sky that I kiss,
and this land that I touch
and sings in my hands;
with centuries of civilization
under its feet.

Sicily has no longer a name:
but millions of deaf and mutes
cast down inside a well
whom I call but they can't hear,
and if I stretch my arms,
they bite my hands.

I'd lower my veins as ropes,
the nets of the eyes
to pull them out of the well;
because here I was born
and I speak my father's language;
and the fish,
the birds,

u ventu,
puru u ventu!
trasi nt'aricchi
e ciarlaria nsicilianu.

Cca nascivu,
e si mi vasu i manu
vasu i manu di me morti;
e si m'asciucu l'occhi
asciucu l'occhi di me morti.

Cca nascivu,
addattavu nte minni di sta terra,
ci sucavu u sangu:
si mi tagghiati i vini,
vi bruciati i manu!

Non è veru c'amamu a Sicilia
si avemu a storia nto pugnu
e l'affucamu;
non è veru
si addumanu u focu
e l'astutamu;
non è veru mancu
si stamu un ghiornu libiri
e pi cent'anni servi.

Non dumannamu pirdunu a storia
ora ca nni scurdamu
i martiri di tutti i tempi
ca misiru u coddu sutta a mannara
senza chianciri:
Di Blasi, unu![1]

1 Francesco Paolo di Blasi, giacobino, decapitato nel 1795.

the wind,
yes, even the wind!
enters my ears
and chatters in Sicilian.

Here I was born,
and if I kiss my hands
I'm kissing the hands of my dead.
and if I dry my eyes
I'm drying the eyes of my dead.

Here I was born,
I suckled the milk of this land,
I suckled its blood:
if you sever my veins
your hands will be burned!

It's not true that we love Sicily
if its history is in our fist
and we drown it;
it is not true
if we light a fire
and extinguish it;
it's not even true
if for one day we're free
and slaves a hundred years.

Let's not ask history for mercy
now that we forget
the martyrs of all ages
who placed their necks under the butcher ax
without crying:
Di Blasi was one of them.[1]

1 Francesco Paolo di Blasi, accused of subversive activities and decapitated in 1795.

Ora ca nni scurdamu
i torturati nte galeri,
i cunnannati a vita,
i nfurcati,
e l'arrustuti vivi nte chiazzi.

Petri e fangu
pi cu supporta a miseria,
petri e fangu
pi cu batti i manu e putenti
petri e fangu
pi cu non metti u coddu
nta furca da libirtà:
u dicu e siciliani,
e mi scatta u cori!

E fu aeri,
(a data non cunta)
io vitti chianciri i matri
nto Chianu da Purtedda,
e Saveria Megna
addinucchiata supra l'erba
parrari cu so figghiu ammazzatu.

Idda u videva,
io no:
u foddi era io
si doppu vitti nesciri di fossi
tutti i morti
pa libirtà da Sicilia:
vivi
a migghiara
a marusi
cu focu nta l'occhi!

Now that we forget
those tortured in jail,
those sentenced for life,
those hung on the gallows,
those burned alive in the squares.

Stones and mud
for those who tolerate poverty,
stones and mud
for those who applaud the powerful,
stones and mud
for those who do not place their necks
in the gallows of liberty:
I say this to Sicilians,
and my heart breaks!

And it was yesterday,
(the date doesn't matter)
I saw mothers weeping
on the Plain of the Purtedda,
and Saveria Megna,
kneeling on the grass
speaking to her dead son.

She saw him,
I didn't:
I was the fool
if afterward I saw all those
who died for freedom in Sicily
emerge from their graves:
alive
by the thousands
like waves
with fire in their eyes!

Dammi la manu
Cola Lumbardu,[2]
(io parrava cu iddu!')
sfardati a cammisa, ci dissi,
fammi vìdiri i pirtusa nto pettu
sfunnatu di baddi taliani.
A Bronti, ci, dissi,
nto Chianu i San Vitu
dopu cent'anni cu passa
senti ancora a tò vuci:
moru pu populu!

Cuntami a storia
Turiddu Carnivali,
(io parrava cu iddu!')
figghiu du nfernu e du paradisu,
cuntami a storia!
Nta stu pugnu c'è a morti,
ti dissiru;
nta stu pugnu i dinari,
ti dissiru;

e tu:
a morti,
a morti!
E ci turcisti u pugnu.

L'indumani
a Sciara
i cumpagni
u purtavanu a spadda:
quattru,
sudati,
un passu doppu l'àutru.

2 Avvocato, fucilato per ordine di Nino Bixio, il giorno 8 Agosto 1860, per avere capeggiato una sommossa di contadini che chiedevano la ripartizione delle terre.

Give me your hand,
Cola Lumbardu [2]
(I was talking to him)
Tear your shirt I said to him,
let me see the holes in your chest,
pierced by Italian bullets.
In Bronte, I said to him,
in the plain of San Vitu.
after a hundred years, whoever passes
can still hear your voice:
I am dying for the people!
Tell me your story,

Turiddu Carnivali,
(I was talking with him!)
son of hell and paradise,
tell me your story!
In this fist there is death.
they said to you;
in this fist there is money,
they said to you;

and you replied:
death,
death!
And you twisted their fist.

The next day
at Sciara
the comrades
carried him on their shoulders:
four,
sweating,
one step after the other.

2 A lawyer who was shot on orders by Nino Bixio, on August 8, 1860, for leading a peasant revolt. They were asking for the land distribution promised by Garibaldi.

Ntutt'unu
a cascia
divintò leggia,
ci scappava di nmanu
u mortu un c'era nta cascia,
caminava in prima fila
nmenzu i banneri russi;
a testa,
tuccava u celu!

Cu camina calatu
torci a schina,
s'è un populu
torci a storia.

Then suddenly
the coffin
became light,
it slid from their hands
the dead man was no longer in the coffin,
he was walking in the first row
surrounded by red flags;
his head
touched the sky!

Whoever walks bowed,
just bends his spine,
if it's a people
it bends history.

Lingua e dialettu

(Da *Io faccio il poeta*)

Un populu
mittitilu a catina
spugghiatilu
attuppatici a vucca,
è ancora libiru.

Livatici u travagghiu
u passaportu
a tavula unni mancia
u lettu unni dormi,
è ancora riccu.

Un populu,
diventa poviru e servu,
quannu ci arrobbanu a lingua
addutata di patri:
è persu pi sempri.

Diventa poviru e servu,
quannu i paroli non figghianu paroli
e si mancianu tra d'iddi.
Mi nn' addugnu ora,
mentri accordu a chitarra du dialettu
ca perdi na corda lu jornu.

Mentri arripezzu
a tila camuluta
chi tisseru i nostri avi
cu lana di pecuri siciliani.

E sugnu poviru:
haiu i dinari
e non li pozzu spènniri;

Language and Dialect

Put a people in chains,
strip them naked,
plug up their mouths,
they are still free;

take away their passports
the place where they eat,
the bed where they sleep,
they are still rich.

A people become
poor and enslaved
when you rob them of their tongue
handed down by their forefathers:
they are lost forever.

They become poor and enslaved
when their words
don't father other words
and they devour one another.
I realize it now,
as I tune my dialect guitar
that is losing
a string every day.

As I patch up
the worm-eaten tapestry
our ancestors wove
with wool of Sicilian sheep.

And I am poor,
I have money
but I cannot spend it;

i giuelli
e non li pozzu rigalari;
u cantu nta gaggia
cu l'ali tagghiati.
Un poviru,
c' addatta nte minni strippi
da matri putativa,
chi u chiama figghiu
pi nciuria.

Nuàtri l' avevamu a matri,
nni l'arrubbaru;
aveva i minni a funtani di latti
e ci vìppiru tutti,
ora ci sputanu.

Nni ristò a vuci d'idda,
a cadenza,
a nota vascia
du sonu e du lamentu:
chissi non nni ponnu rubari.

Nni ristò a sumigghianza,
l'annatura,
i gesti,
i lampi nta l'occhi:
chissi non nni ponnu rubari.
Non nni ponnu rubari,
ma ristamu poviri
e orfani u stissu.

Gennaio 1970

I have jewels
and I can't give them away;
the song inside a cage,
with its wings chopped off.
Like a poor man sucking
at the withered teat
of a putative mother
who calls him son
as a way of mocking him.

We had a mother once,
She was stolen from us;
her breasts were fountains of milk
and all once drank from them,
now they spit on them.

Her voice has remained,
her cadence,
that deep low note
of the sound and the lament.
No one can steal these from us.

We bear her resemblance,
the way she walked,
her gestures,
the lightning flashes in our eyes.
No one can steal these from us.
No one can steal them,
but we remain poor,
and orphans, just the same.

January 1970

Li pirati a Palermu

(Da *Lu trenu di lu suli*)

Arrivaru li navi
tanti navi a Palermu,
li pirati sbarcaru
cu li facci di nfernu.
Nn'arrubbaru lu suli,
Arristamu a lu scuru,
Sicilia, chianci!
lu suli!
chi scuru!
Tuttu l'oru all'aranci
li pirati arrubbaru,
li campagni spugghiati
cu la negghia lassaru.
Nn'arrubbaru lu suli,
lu suli!
Arristamu a lu scuru,
chi scuru!
Sicilia, chianci!
Li culura a lu mari
nn'arrubbaru, chi ddannu!
Su' mpazzuti li pisci,
chi lamentu chi fannu!
Nn'arrubbaru lu suli,
lu suli!
Arristamu a lu scuru,
chi scuru!
Sicilia, chianci!
A li fimmini nostri
ci scipparu di l'occhi
la lustrura e lu focu
c'addumava li specchi!
Nn'arrubbaru lu suli,
lu suli!

The Pirates in Palermo

The ships have landed
in Palermo,
so many ships,
the pirates disembarked
with faces straight from hell.
They have stolen our sun
we are left in the dark,
Sicily weeps!
our Sun!
what darkness!
All the gold from our oranges
the pirates have stolen,
our gardens stripped bare
they have left in the fog.
They have stolen our Sun,
our Sun!
We are left in the dark,
what darkness!
Sicily weeps!
The colors from the sea
they have stolen, oh what harm!
The fish are in a frenzy,
how woefully they cry!
They have stolen our Sun,
our Sun!
We are left in the dark,
what darkness!
Sicily weeps.
They have stolen the fire
from the eyes of our women,
the brightness that mirrors lit up!
They have stolen our Sun,
our Sun!

Arristamu a lu scuru,
chi scuru!
Sicilia, chianci!

We are left in the dark,
what darkness!
Sicily weeps.

U rancuri
Discorso ai feudatari

(Da *Io faccio il poeta*)

Chi mi cuntati?
io u pueta fazzu!
C'è aria di timpesta
u sacciu,
a vidu:
u marusu sata i scogghi,
u celu avvampa!

Chi mi cuntati?
iu a paci amu;
e sta casa facci u mari
cu Palermu nte vrazza,
i muntagni ntesta,
e l'aceddi ca passanu e salutanu.

Vuàtri nte città,
nte palazzi moderni
chi cammareri in divisa;
chi fimmini in vestaglia,
beddi,
e i minni duri.
Nte palazzi e nte città,
quagghiati du piaciri;
chi cani e chi gatti
ca sàtanu nte gammi,
chi ghiocanu nte divani;
chi mancianu comu vuàtri
e cacanu nte gnuni.

Io vi cunsidiru,
e forsi
arrivu a scusarivi:
u privilegiu piaci,

Rancor
To the Estate Owners

What are you telling me?
I am a poet!
There's a storm brewing
I know,
I see it.
The breakers jump over the rocks,
the sky is on fire!

What are you telling me?
I love peace;
and this house facing the sea
with Palermo in its arms,
the mountains overhead
and birds that greet me as they pass.

And you are in the city,
living in modern buildings,
waiters in uniform,
women in lounging gowns,
beautiful,
and with hard breasts.
In the palaces and cities,
wallowing in pleasures,
with dogs and cats
that jump upon your legs,
playing on sofas
eating at your tables
and shitting in the corners.

I see your side
and maybe
I manage to excuse you:
privilege is a good thing

a tradizioni di l'abusu
a disumanità
u sfruttamentu piaci,
l'aviti nto sangu;
e vurissivu ristari a cavaddu
cu elmu e scutu
e li spati puntati;
crociati di l'ingiustizia,
a massacrari i poveri.

Io vi cunsidiru,
haiu a facci tosta!
sunnu i braccianti chi v'odianu,
i disoccupati a turnu;
all'asta nte chiazzi
ad aspittari un patruni
chi pritenni lu baciulimanu.
Sunnu i senzaterra,
i cozzi cotti o suli chi v'odianu,
vonnu i feudi:
u vostru sangu sigillatu nte carti,
un orbu ci leggi!
I feudi,
chi taliati cu cannocchiali
e nàtanu nta l'aria.

Sunnu latri!
Non lu dicu io
iddi u dicinu:
"Semu latri,
nnu nzignastivu vuàtri."
Non lu dicu io
iddi u dicinu:
"I nostri nanni
i nanni di nostri nanni
i nostri patri
si susevanu all'arba;

the tradition of abuse,
the inhumanity,
exploitation pleases,
you have in your blood;
and you would like to stay on top
with shields and helmets
and swords at the ready;
crusaders of injustice,
to massacre the poor.

I see your side,
I am brazen!
It's the laborers who hate you,
the unemployed on line,
at auction in the squares,
waiting for an owner
who expects them to kiss his hand.
It's those who have no land,
with necks scorched by the sun who hate you,
they want the land in your estates:
your blood sealed in the papers,
a blind man reads for them!
The estates
that you survey with binoculars
and swim in air.

They are thieves!
It's not me saying this.
They say it:
"We are thieves,
you are the ones who taught us."
It's not me saying this.
They say it:
"Our grandfathers
our great grandfathers
our fathers
got up at dawn,

facevano a strata a pedi,
turnavanu cu scuru,
durmevanu quattr'uri.

Vuàtri aviti a dòrmiri quattr'uri
zappari quattordici uri
disidirari u pani
torciri i cammìsi
stricari u mussu nterra
sputari u sangu di primuna,
vuàtri!

Vuàtri aviti a strinciri ossa di fimmina
sunnàri miseria
lamenti
dispirazioni;
darivi pugna ntesta,
vuàtri!"

Non lu dicu io
iddi u dicinu:
"Si niscissiru di fossi
i nostri morti
vi nfurcassiru;
v'abbruciassiru vivi!

Vi mittissiru u capizzuni
u sidduni
u suttapanza
i spiruna a valanza
i muschi cavaddini;
e lignati nte rini,
nte rini!"

Non lu dicu io
iddi u dicinu:
"Facevanu i guerri,

and walked to work on foot,
returning home at dusk,
and sleeping for four hours."

You're the ones who should sleep four hours,
hoe in the field for fourteen hours,
longing for a piece of bread
twisting your shirt dry,
rubbing the ground with your mouth,
spitting blood from your lungs,
you are the ones!

You're the ones who must squeeze women's bones,
dream of poverty
laments
desperation;
land blows upon your heads,
you!"

It's not me saying this.
They say it:
"If our dead people
came out of their graves
they'd string you on the gallows,
they would burn you alive!

They would put halters on you
a pack on your back
an underbelly strap
spurs in pairs
horseflies
and blows on your kidneys,
on your kidneys!

It's not me saying this.
They say it:
"They waged wars

(i faciti ancora
e poveri di dintra
ed e populi di fora)
u re mannava a cartullina,
urdinava a mobilitazioni;
i matri accumpagnavanu
i figghi a stazioni,
i muggheri u maritu;
i picciriddi chiancevanu,
e vuàtri battevavu i manu.
Arrivavanu o campu,
u ginirali faceva a parlata;
u parrinu diceva a missa,
dava i santuzzi,
l'infirvurava:
'Cu mori cca,
acchiana ncelu,'
e ghisava u iditu.

U diceva apposta;
i morti ristavano suttaterra,
scattavano;
i fimmini si vistevanu a luttu,
si scurciavanu l'ossa;
mmaledicevanu u nfernu,
u paradisu;
i figghi
taliavanu u ritrattu o muru,
u ritrattu du guardianu da casa,
mortu."

Non lu dicu io
iddi u dicinu:
"Ci facevavu u monumentu,
ci scrivevavu l'epigrafi:
nomi
cugnomi

(you still do
against poor people here
and the people outside)
the king would send a card
to mobilize for war;
mothers accompanied
their children to the trains
wives accompanied husbands;
the children the would cry,
and you applauded.
When they arrived to camp,
the general made a speech,
the priest said mass,
giving images of saints,
to stir them on:
'Those who die here,
go straight to heaven,'
and raised his finger.

He said that in jest;
the dead remained underground,
they burst;
the women wore black in mourning,
peeling flesh from their bones;
cursing hell,
paradise;
the children
gazed at the portrait on the wall,
the portrait of the guardian of the house,
now dead."

It's not me saying this.
They say it:
"You made monuments for them,
you wrote epigraphs for them:
first name
last name

gradu:
Morti per la patria."

Sgràccanu na bistemia:
"Morti pi patruna!
Pi porci grassi!
Pi lupi!"

Non lu dicu io
iddi u dicinu:
"Fineva a guerra,
i vivi turnavanu;
l'orbi
i surdi
i muti,
i pazzi turnavanu;
turnavanu chiddi chi gammi tagghiati,
i sfriggiati,
i senzavrazza;
ci appizzavanu i midagghi,
– i frattagghi o pettu –
e i facevanu sfilari;
a banna sunava:
viva u re!
viva u re!
e vuàtri battevavu i manu."

Non lu dicu io
iddi u dicinu:
certi voti chiancinu,
si muzzicanu i manu;
io mi cummovu.
"Turnavanu nte tani" dicinu,
"Turnavanu a manciari erba,
a scaricari varrìla di suduri,
a marinari cunigghi magri;
i cunigghi figghiavanu cunigghi,

rank:
They died for the motherland."

They spit out a blasphemy:
"They died for the landowners!
For the fat pigs!
For the wolves!"

It's not me saying this.
They say it:
"The war then ended:
those living returned;
the blind,
the deaf,
the mute,
the mad returned;
those with no legs returned,
the disfigured,
those with no arms;
they hung medals on them,
—giblets for their chests—
and made them march in parades
with a band playing:
long live the king!
Long live the king!
And you applauded."

It's not me saying this.
They say it:
sometimes they cry,
sometimes the bite their hands,
I am moved.
"They returned to their caves," they say,
"they went back to eating grass,
to unload barrels of sweat,
to impregnate skinny rabbits;
the rabbit produced more rabbits,

l'erba non bastava.

Si niscevanu di tani
cu l'ugna i fora,
cu ritrattu du re,
chi banneri tricculura;
chi picciriddi nte crapicchi
c'addattavanu sucu d'erba amara,
si scatinava a carnificina;
ci mannavanu i carrubineri,
i surdati italiani
a sparari supra i scheletri:
addumavanu cu un cirinu,
fitevanu nte chiazzi!

Vineva u carruzzuni,
arricuggheva a munnizza,
u parrinu a binidiceva:
requièscat in pace,
e a munnizza acchianava ncelu.

Ncelu si riuniva a 'Corti':
giurati
magistrati
presidenti,
e facevanu u prucessu:
ascutavanu a parti lesa,
i testimoni,
a difisa:
nisceva a sintenza,
assolti!

Cumparevanu l'ancili;
l'ancili ci mpristavanu l'ali,
San Petru grapeva i porti,
e a munnizza traseva mparadisu."

but grass was not enough.

If they emerged from their caves
with nails at the ready
with the king's portrait,
with the tricolored flags,
with children stuck to nipples
that sucked the juice of bitter grass,
a massacre would occur;
you'd summon the police,
Italian soldiers came
to shoot the skeletons:
they burned with just a match
that made squares stink.

A heavy cart would come
to gather all the garbage,
the priest would bless it:
requiescat in pace,
and the garbage rose to heaven.

In heaven the Court assembled
jurors
magistrates,
the president,
and they'd begin the trial:
they listened to the accusers
the witnesses
the defense
the sentence then was read:
not guilty!

The angels would appear;
the angels lent them wings,
Saint Peter opened the gates,
and the garbage entered paradise."

Non lu dicu io
iddi u dicinu.
Io u pueta fazzu:
caminu supra i negghi,
leggiu nto celu,
cuntu i stiddi,
parru ca luna:
acchianu
e scinnu!
U pueta fazzu:
tessu,
raccamu,
cusu,
scusu:
arripezzu cu fili d'oru!

Adornu, allisciu, allustru:
decoru senza culuri!
Ntrizzu ciuri,
appàru artari,
chiantu banneri:
abbillisciu u munnu,
carmu u mari ca vuci!

Sugnu un ghiardinu di ciuri
e mi spartu a tutti;
una cassa armonica
e sonu pi tutti;
un agneddu smammatu
e chianciu pi tutti agneddi smammati.

Chi mi cuntati?
io u pueta fazzu:
amu i tavuli cunzati,
i fimmini,
i piacìri,
u lussu.

It's not me saying this.
They say it:
I am a poet:
I walk above the clouds,
I read in the sky,
I count the stars,
I talk with the moon,
I climb up
and down!
I am a poet by profession:
I spin,
I embroider,
I sew,
unsew,
I mend with golden threads!

I adorn, I smooth, I polish:
I decorate without colors!
I arrange flowers,
I set up altars,
I plant banners:
I beautify the world;
I calm the sea with my voice!

I am a flower garden
and share myself with all;
a sound-box
and I play for all;
a weaned lamb
and I weep for all weaned lambs.

What are you telling me?
I am a poet:
I love set dinner tables
women,
pleasures,
luxuries.

Amu i dinari
(a bumma atomica nte manu di l'omu,
nto cori di l'omu
e nun scatta!)

U pueta fazzu,
e vogghiu a paci nta me casa
pi scurdari a guerra
nte casi di l'àutri;
a cuitutini nta me casa
pi scurdari u tirrimotu
nte casi di l'àutri:
sugnu un cani da vostra razza!

Non mi manca nenti,
non disidiru nenti;
sulu na curuna
pi recitari u rusariu a sira,
e nun c'è nuddu
chi me la porta di ferru filatu
pi nchiacchiarimi a un palu!

I love money
(the atomic bomb in the hands of man,
in the heart of man
and does not blow!)

I am a poet,
and I want peace inside my home
to forget the war
in other people's homes;
quietude in my home
to forget the earthquake
in other people's homes:
I am a dog of your same breed!

I lack nothing,
I want nothing;
only a crown
to recite the rosary at night
and there's no one
who'll bring me one made of spun iron
so I can hang myself down from a pole.

Nun mi lassari sulu

(Da *Io faccio il poeta*)

Ascutami,
parru a tia stasira
e mi pari di parrari o munnu.

Ti vogghiu diri
di non lassàrimi sulu
nta sta strata longa
chi non finisci mai
ed havi i jorna curti.

Ti vogghiu diri
chi quattr'occhi vidinu megghiu,
chi miliuna d'occhi
vidinu chiù luntanu,
e chi lu pisu spartutu nte spaddi
diventa chiù leggìu.

Ti vogghiu diri
ca si t'appoji a mia
e io m appoju a tia
non putemu cadiri
mancu si lu furturati
nn'assicutanu a vintati.
L'aceddi volanu a sbardu,
cantanu a sbardu,
nu cantu sulu è lamentu
e mori ntall'aria.

Non calari l'occhi,
ti vogghiu amicu a tavula;
e non è vero mai
ca si diversu di mia
c'allongu i vrazza
e ti chiamu: frati...

Don't Leave Me All Alone

Listen to me,
tonight, I want to talk to you
but I think I'm talking to the world.

I want to tell you
not to leave me all alone
on this long journey
that never seems to end,
while its days are short.

I want to tell you
that four eyes see better,
and that a million eyes
see even farther,
and that a weight that's shared upon our shoulders
becomes much lighter.

I want to tell you
that if you lean on me,
and I then lean on you,
we can't fall down,
not even if we're chased
by gusts in a windstorm.
Birds fly together in a flock,
they sing in chorus,
a solitary song is a lament
and fades away in air.

Don't lower your eyes.
I want you as a friend at my table.
It's never true that you
are different from me,
who extend my arms
and call you: brother…

Frati ti sugnu e cumpagnu
calatu a scippari i spini
chi nsangunianu i pedi:
frati e cumpagnu jisatu
a sfardari i negghi
e astutari i lampi:
frati e cumpagnu
si scattanu i trona
e trema a terra,
si spunta u suli e l' abbrazza.

Unu non fa numiru,
nascemu pi cantari nzemmula
e non pi lassari
eredità di lacrimi
e ripitiu di lamenti.
Si mori
e si resta a nàtari
nto lettu du ciumi
chi scìddica a mari,
nto lettu chi cunta
la storia di sempri.

E sarannu jorna
comu chisti:
cu l'arba e lu suli
i gaddi chi cantanu
l'arbuti chi ciuriscinu,
l'omini nterra
e miliardi di stiddi nto celu.

Jorna comu chisti:
cu lustru nte strati
chi tavuli cunzati
chi picciriddi chi ghiocanu,
e l'amuri nte letti
ca vucca d' agneddu e di lupu.

I am your brother, your comrade,
bending to remove thorns
that bloody your feet:
brother and comrade, standing
to chase away the fog
and extinguish lightnings:
brother and comrade
in case there's thunder
snd the earth shakes
and if the sun rises and embraces it.

One man amounts to nothing,
we were born to sing together
and not to leave behind
a legacy of tears
and a litany of laments.
We die
and we remain swimming
in the river bed
that flows toward the sea,
in the bed that relates
ever the same tale.

And there will be days
like these:
with a sunrise and dawn,
with roosters singing,
trees blossoming,
and men on earth
and billions of stars in the sky.

Days like these:
with light in the streets
and tables set up
with children playing
and lovemaking in bed,
with mouths of lambs and wolves.

Jorna comu chisti:
cu tia e cu mia
chiamati cu àutri nomi
a cunsultari libri,
a spirimintari,
a giudicari i vivi e i morti
si miritamu pirdunu.
Pirdunu pi guerri a catina
pi stragi
pi Hiroshima bruciata
pi pueti fucilati.

Pirdunu pi càmmari a gas
pi l'ingiustizia codificata,
pu nfernu addumatu
nto paradisu da terra,
pi Cristu ncruci
e lu boia a l'artaru.

Mi staju cunfissannu ...
Cu m'assolvi?
Cu t'assolvi?
A storia no,
si putemu fari
a guerra paci
u chiantu gioia
a schiavitù libirtà
l'odiu amuri,
e non lu facemu.

Si putemu abbattiri
i mura di petra d'ossa
chi ghisamu ogni ghiornu
chi manu lordi,
tu e io chi manu lordi,
e non lu facemu.

Days like these:
with you and me
called by other names
consulting books,
experimenting,
judging the living and the dead
If we deserve forgiveness.
Forgiveness for unending wars
for the massacres
for the burned Hiroshima
for poets shot.

Forgiveness for the gas chambers
for the codified injustice,
for kindling the hell
on the paradise of earth,
for Christ on the Cross
and for the executioner on the altar.

I'm making a confession…
Who will absolve me?
Who will absolve you?
History won't,
If we can make
peace out of war
turn weeping into joy,
slavery into freedom,
hatred into love
and we do not do it.

If we can crush
the stony walls of bones
that we raise each day
with dirty hands,
you and me, with dirty hands,
and we do not do it.

Mi staju cunfissannu.
A storia no,
si putemu mpastari
u distinu di l' omini
cu farina bianca:
si putemu tagghiari
i riticulati du disprezzu
di la nvidia
da crudiltà,
e non lu facemu.

Si io tu e tutti
cu un ghiditu;
(grapi a manu)
unu,
putissimu scippari
i radichi marci
chi mpestanu a terra,
e non lu f acemu.

Si io e tu
e cu mi senti e non mi senti,
cu un ciusciuni;
(grapi a vucca e fa ventu)
cu un ciusciuni
putissimu sdirrubbari
i càrciri da libirtà
i pinitinziarii di l' amuri
i lazzaretti di scartati
i cimineri ca fumanu sònnira,
e non lu facemu.

Io non dormu sonni sireni
tu non dormi sonni sireni,
e m'arruspigghianu gridi
di guerra e lamenti
sbattuti a la finestra.

I am making a confession.
History won't,
if we can knead
the destiny of men
with white flour:
if we can cut
the fences of disdain
of envy
of cruelty,
and we do not do it.

If I, you, and everyone
with one finger
(open your hand)
one,
could tear out
the rotten roots
that pollute the earth
and we do not do it.

If I and you
and whoever listens to me
but does not hear me
with just one breath;
(open your mouth and blow)
with just one breath
could destroy the prisons of freedom
the penitentiaries of love
the lazarets of the outcasts,
the chimneys that smoke dreams
and we do not do it.

I don't sleep peacefully at night,
you don't sleep peacefully at night,
and shouts of war and moans
crashing against the window
awaken me.

E l'arba di paci
c'aspettu ogni ghiornu,
cu l'occhi d'orbu,
chiovi sangu.

And the dawn of peace
that I await each day
with a blind man's eyes
drips blood.

Cumpagni di viaggiu

(Da *Io faccio il poeta*)

Stasira li cimi di l'arbuli
chi mòvinu la testa e li vrazza
parranu d'amuri a la terra
e io li sentu.

Sunnu li paroli di sempri
chi vui scurdastivu,
cumpagni di viaggiu
nudi e pilusi,
in transitu dintra gaggi di ferru.

Unn'è chi ghiti a càdiri
si nuddu v'accumpagna
e la scienza è in guerra contru l'omu?

Cu vi jetta li riti
mentri u marusu munta;
siddu i nostromi da puisia
un tempu piscatura di baleni,
ora piscanu a lenza
nni l'acqua marcia di li paludi?

Cumpagni di viaggiu,
si pirdistivu u cori pa strata;
turnati nnarreri a circallu
si non siti già orbi.

Si u suttirrastuvu chi morti
nte campi di battagghia;
jiti a svrudicallu
si non feti nto sangu.

Si ristò a bruciari
nte càmmiri a gas;

Travel Companions

Tonight the tops of trees
that sway their heads and arms
speak of their love for earth
and I can hear them.

They're always the same words
you have forgotten,
my travel companions
naked and hairy,
transiting in iron cages.

Where will you ever land
if no one is escorting you
and science wages war against mankind?

Who will throw out the nets to you
when breakers will surge high;
if the boatswains of poetry
who hunted whales before
are now throwing their lines
in putrid waters of the marsh?

Travel companions,
if you lost your heart on the way,
go back and try to find it,
if you are not already blind.

If you buried it with the dead
down in the fields of battle,
go to dig it out
if it does not smell in the blood.

If it was left to burn
inside the gas chambers,

curriti a cogghiri a cìnniri
e mittitila a cuvari nto pettu.

Lu me straziu è pi vui stasira,
e li paroli d'amuri
càdinu nterra
comu stiddi astutati.

Non vurrìa chi mai turnassi
una sira la stissa.

run to collect the ashes
and place them in your chest to brood.

My anguish is for you tonight,
and for my words of love
falling to the ground
like faded stars.

I never want to see
another night like this.

Si mori dui voti

(Da *Io faccio il poeta*)

Li paroli boni
cari e umani
custanu nenti
e non sacciu pirchì
l'omini li sparagnanu.

Li paroli di cunfortu
ca medicanu u duluri,
e dunanu tempu o cori d'abbacari
e a menti di ripusari,
nni quagghianu nte vucchi
e nn'agghiuttemu amari.

La buntà,
c'agghiorna i facci
e pitta arcubaleni
nto celu di l'occhi,
l'ammucciamu nte negghi
prima di nasciri.

E nn'avemu bisognu
io e vuàtri
ca criditi u pueta
un dumanneri di pezzi vecchi;
mentri cusi mantelli cilesti
chi manu di matri
pi quadiari u munnu.

Tutti nn'avemu bisognu,
comu a terra malata
c'addimanna acqua
cu a gula sicca:
comu u celu
c'ammustra a facci lavata

We Die twice

Good words
tender and human words
cost nothing
and I don't know why
people use them so sparingly.

Words of comfort
that heal pain,
and give the heart time to calm down
and to the mind some rest,
freeze in our mouths
and we swallow bitterness.

Goodness,
that dawns on our faces
and paints rainbows
in the sky of the eyes,
we hide in the fog
before it is born.

And we have need of it
I and you
who think that a poet
is a beggar of used cothes
while he sews celestial robes
with the hands of a mother
to warm the world.

We all need it,
like the sick earth
begging for water
with a parched throat:
like the sky
that shows a washed face

e stenni linzola
si lu ventu stramina li negghi.

Ed è inutili strinciri i denti
e attirantari li vrazza;
u marusu acchiana u stissu,
arrivota l'unni,
sbatti nte scogghi du pettu.

Basta na taliata, a li voti,
na magia di l'occhi,
na sbuccata du cori
p'arrivisciri un mortu chi chianci.

L'omini u sannu,
sannu parrari
cu cori nta l'occhi
e non lu fannu:
l'usanu pi ngfinnari,
pi cuvari odiu,
pi chiantari furchi.

Parru cu cori prenu
e cu scantu chi sgravassi
i me dogghi di pirsiguitatu,
di diavula nta chesa,
d'agneddu scannatu;
di ugnati
nte carni tenniri di picciriddu
ed arrappati d'oggi:
u feli m'acchiana a vucca!

Ed è pi tantu disfiziu
si sacciu sulu chianciri e sfardari
sti fogghi di carta
ca sunnu bianchi
e mi pàrinu nìvuri;

and hangs bedsheets
if the wind disperses the fogs.

And it is useless
to grind your teeth.
and tighten your arms.
The breakers swell any way, churning the waves
that crash on the rocks of the heart.

A look alone suffices, sometimes,
a magic glance of the eyes,
a word from the heart
to resurrect a dead man crying.

Men know this,
they know how to talk
with the heart in their eyes
and they don't do it:
they use it to deceive,
to harbor hatred,
to raise gallows.

I speak with a heavy heart
and with the fear might unload
my woes as a persecuted man,
of devils in a church,
of a slaughtered lamb;
of nail scratches
on my tender flesh as child
and on my wrinkled flesh today:
gall rises in my mouth!

And it's because of so much bitterness
that I know only how to cry and consume
these sheets of paper
that are white
but seem black to me;

si cercu cunsolu
nta n' aceddu chi canta,
(poviru Saba!)
nta un cani chi m'aspetta;
nta na parola d' amuri
rubata o ventu,
caduta du celu,
piscata nto funnu du mari.

Non mi diciti
chi tuttu è pirdutu,
vi pregu:
si mori dui voti.

Aspittati dumani,
dumani,
ogni ghiornu, dumani!

if I seek consolation
in a singing bird.
(poor Saba!)
in a dog that waits for me;
in a word of love
stolen from the wind,
fallen from the sky,

fished out from the bottom of the sea.
Don't tell me
that all is lost,
I beg of you:
we die twice.

Wait for tomorrow,
tomorrow,
every day, tomorrow.

U latti da matri

(Da *Io faccio il poeta*)

Io non sugnu campusantaru pirchì penzu
ca i morti non parranu
ed hannu tanti cosi di dirinni.

Nuàtri sì;
addinucchiati supra i fossi
nni scarricamu di paroli;
li videmu vivi;
ci cuntamu
a nostra vita disgraziata
di quannu nni lassaru.

Ci dicemu,
ca non nni putemu scurdari;
ca li chiamamu nto sonnu;
ma i morti non sentinu,
non vidinu,
ed hannu l'occhi aperti.

Siddu i morti
sintissiru e parrassiru
quantu cosi dicissi a me matri;
non pi fariccinni curpa,
(ca vurrissi c'arriviscissi
e farimi chiù mali di prima) ;
ma pi sapiri
pirchì nta sissant'anni
non mi tinni mai nto pettu
e non mi vasò mai di figghiu.

Io penzu
ca i matri,
tutti i matri,
dùnanu cu latti

A Mother's Milk

I'm not one for graveyards because I think
that the dead do not talk
and have a lot to say to us.

But we do talk,
kneeling over the graves.
we unload ourselves of words,
we see them alive;
we tell them about
our lives plagued by misfortunes,
since when they left us.

We tell them
that we cannot forget them,
we call them in our dreams.
But the dead cannot hear,
they cannot see,
and their eyes are open.

If the dead
could hear and speak,
how many things would I say to my mother!
Not to blame her for her faults
(for I want her to wake up again
so she could hurt me more than then)
but to find out
why in my sixty years
she never held me to her breast
and never kissed me as a son.

I think
that mothers
every mother,
give their flesh

a so carni
e u so sangu;
ca a prima stizza di latti
a spreminu du cori,
e chi diventanu mammi
a la prima sucata du figghiu.

Me matri
latti non mi nni detti,
pozzu diri
nascivu orfanu,
m'allattava a balia.

L'amuri pu figghiu,
io penzu,
nasci nta matri
u primu jornu ca u strinci o pettu;
tannu u vidi,
u tocca,
u vasa:
ci pari un miraculu!

Prima no,
u videva cu pìnzeri;
u videva darreri i negghi:
puteva vèniri a timpesta!

U videva nto funnu du mari:
i pisci su putevanu manciari

Ora ci parra
l'accarizza,
u vidi ridiri:
idda canta!

Io
ricordo sulu

and blood
together with their milk
because the first drop of their milk
is squeezed out of their hearts,
and that they become mothers,
when her son first suckles at her breast.

My mother
never gave me of her milk.
I can say
that I was born an orphan.
I was fed by a wet-nurse.

The love for a son,
I think,
is born in mothers
on the first day she holds him to her breast.
That's when she sees him;
touches him
kissing him,
thinking he is a miracle!

Not before.
She saw him in her mind;
she saw him from behind a fog,
even through the storm!

She saw him at the bottom of the sea;
fish could have eaten him alive.

Now she talks to him;
caresses him,
sees him laugh:
she sings!

I
remember only

paroli àciti di me matri,
liti in famigghia,
causi,
nutara;
e la so vuci di patruna
(puntuali ogni misi)
davanti a me porta
a minacciari sfrattu
pi l'affittu scadutu.

Addivintavu vecchiu
senza sapiri
comu vasanu i matri,
comu strincinu i figghi nto pettu
e zoccu sentinu l'ossa:
ci penzu, e tremu!

Addivintavu vecchiu
senza sapiri a cu dallu
l'amuri miu di figghiu
chi lu tempu tirò di lu focu
e lu batti bruciatu
nta ncùnia du me cori.

A cu l'haiu a dari?
I matri sunnu dui,
dui: una fici u nidu,
fici l'ovu di carni,
u cuvò:
(mi toccu e dicu,
ddà era nicu
nto so ventri,)
e strinciu u pugnu.

L'àutra m'allattò,
mi cantò u sonnu,
mi ntisi diri i primi paroli;

bitter words from my mother,
family quarrels,
lawsuits,
lawyers,
and her assertive voice
(every month without fail)
outside my door,
threatening eviction
for late payment of the rent.

I grew old
without knowing
how mothers kiss;
how they embrace their children,
and what they feel inside their bones:
I think of it and shake!

I grew old
without knowing to whom
I should give my filial love
that time drew out of the fire,
and beat it burning upon
the anvil of my heart.

To whom should I give it?
I have two mothers,
two: one made the nest
she made the egg of flesh,
nurtured it:
(I touch myself and say
inside her womb
I was small)
and tighten a fist.

The other nursed me,
sang me to sleep,
heard me mumble my first words;

ridiri e chiànciri
a prima vota:
ciatava cu mia.

L'àutra è cca,
s'incarnò nte me pupiddi,
girìa nta rota di l'occhi:
si la chiamu,
mi senti.

Cu è me matri?

Gennaio 1964

heard me laugh and cry
for the first time.
She breathed with me.

The other is here,
she became flesh inside my pupils,
she turns in the wheeling of my eyes:
if I call her,
she hears me.

Who is my mother?

January 1964

A crucifissioni

(Da *Io faccio il poeta*)

Non ci fu nuddu nta terra
chi parrò comu iddu;
nuddu chi sappi diri paroli
e nsignamenti
pi canciari u distinu di l'omu.

Ed ora è cca
chiantatu a cruci,
vivu e mortu
dopo vinti seculi:
misuratilu cu l'occhi!

Cca
u re di poviri,
u re senza curuna;
u subillaturi chi traviò u munnu
e mmalidiu i putenti.

U malfatturi
ca vosi u mari pi tutti,
u celu pi tutti;
a terra un ghiardinu
pi camminaricci additta
e senza patruni.

Cca
dopu vinti seculi
a rinfacciari o riccu
di campari di pani rubatu:
dacci i robi o sfardatu
ci dici,
i scarpi o scàusu,
a casa o sfrattatu.

The Crucifixion

No one on earth had ever
spoken the way he did;
no one who knew how to express
the words and teachings
to change the destiny of man.

And now he's here
nailed to the cross,
alive and dead
after twenty centuries:
measure him with your eyes.

Here
the king of the poor,
a king without a crown;
a rebel who led the world astray
and cursed the powerful.

The malefactor
who wanted the sea for everyone,
heaven for everyone,
earth as a garden
so all could walk erect
and without masters.

Here
after twenty centuries
to shame the wealthy
for living on stolen bread:
give clothes, he says, to those
whose clothes are worn,
give shoes to the barefooted,
a house to the evicted.

Cca a ripetiri:
vinni pi libirari i servi,
pi dari a ntisa e surdi,
a vista a l'orbi.
Cca a mmalidiri
i scribi e i farisei
ca u lassanu a siccari
affumatu di paroli.

Guardatilu,
u tempu un lu tocca;
e Giuda chi cunta i dinari
nte manu nsangati,
e Pilatu ca i mmustra lavati,
ed Erodi c'acchiana a l'artari.

Guardati u Cireneu
ca s'asciuca u suduri
e nciuria u cunnannatu:
c'aveva sì a facci di galantomu,
ma non ci dissi grazii
p'aviri purtatu dda cruci
cu l'ossa di chiummu.

Guardati u latruni
ca bistimìa e dumanna a grazia
di scìnniri da cruci.

Guardati i surdati
ca sfardanu a tònaca
pi farinni cannavazza.

E chidda è Maria:
dda fimmina abbrazzata a cruci
ca scippa i chiova chi denti,
è Maria:
non pari a matri di Cristu,

Here to repeat:
he came to free the slaves,
to give back hearing to the deaf,
to give sight to the blind.
Here to curse
the scribes and pharisees
who let him wither away
in the smoke of words.

Look at him,
time does not touch him.
And Judas counts his coins
with bloody hands,
and Pilate shows his hands washed clean,
and Herod who's climbing on the altar.

Look at the Cireneum
who wipes his sweat
and curses the condemned:
whose face was of an honest man
but he did not thank him
for carrying that cross
with bones of lead.

Look upon the thief
who curses and asks
to be let down from the cross.

Look at the soldiers
who tear apart the tunic
to make some rags of it.

And that is Mary:
that woman embracing the cross
who's pulling nails out with her mouth,
she is Mary:
She does not look like Christ's mother,

è chiù gàvuta da cruci!
Parra o figghiu vivu:
scinni, ci dici;
scinni da cruci,
torna a casa!

"La me casa è ncelu..."
"È nterra a tò casa,
chiù nica d'un nidu di crita;
ma quannu tu ci trasi, figghiu!
càdinu i mura
e diventa chiù granni di Gerusalemmi".

"Non mi chiamari, figghiu,
non ti chiamari matri..."
"Matri ti sugnu,
t'aduravu novi misi
nta l'artaru du me viddìcu.
mi vasava a panza chi jidita.
M'insignasti a chianciri
prima di nasciri, figghiu!"

"Non mi chiamari, figghiu,
non ti chiamari matri..."
"Matri ti sugnu,
niscisti du me ventri
comu l'oru du focu;
sucasti nta sti minni
di pecura spurpata, figghiu!"

"Non mi chiamari, figghiu,
non ti chiamari matri..."
non vitti mai un figghiu
rinnigari a matri;
non vitti mai u sangu
chioviri di ncelu;
mai na cruci di carni

she's taller than the cross!
Speak to me, living son,
come down, she says to him:
come down from the cross,
come home!

"My house is in Heaven..."
"Your house is here on earth,
smaller than a nest of clay,
but when you enter it, my son,
the walls will fall down
becoming bigger than Jerusalem."

"Don't call me son,
don't call yourself a mother..."
"I am your mother,
I adored you for nine months
in the altar of my belly.
I used to kiss my stomach with my fingers.
You taught me how to cry
before you were born, my son!"

"Don't call me son,
don't call yourself a mother..."
"I am your mother,
you came out from my womb
like the gold of fire,
you suckled at these teats
of this fleshless sheep, my son!"

"Don't call me son,
don't call yourself a mother..."
"I never saw a son
renege his mother;
I never saw blood
raining from the sky,
never a cross of flesh

divintari lignu:
tirrimotu, tirrimotu nterra!"

Silenziu,
cala l'ancilu...
Lu viditi?
"Virgini santa e matri biata,
missaggeru divinu
scinnutu di lu celu
vegnu a cunsulariti."
"Non mi chiamari biata,
chiamami matri disgraziata!
Tu mi dicisti
sugnu l'ancilu Gabrieli
e vegnu a dàriti annunziu
ca pi virtù du Spiritu Santu
u tò ventri parturisci un figghiu
distinatu o tronu di Diu.

E io ti dissi
ca sugnu fimmina di carni e ossa
e si un m'accoppiu a l'omu
non pò nasciri l'agneddu divinu.

E tu mi dicisti
ca nenti è mpussibili a Diu
ca criò u celu e a terra,
l'omu da crita,
e a fimmina
di un ossu da costa d'Adamu."

"Io ti dissi,
sugnu l'ancilu Gabrieli
scinnutu di lu celu
pi vuliri di Diu..."
"Tu non mi dicisti
ca l'avissiru cunnannatu

becoming wood:
earthquake, earthquake on earth!"

"Silence,
the angel's coming down...
Do you see him?
"Holy Virgin, Blessed Mother,
divine messenger
descended from heaven
I came to comfort you."
"Do not call me blessed,
call me an ill-starred mother!
You told me
I am the angel Gabriel
and I came to announce
that by the virtue of the Hoy Ghost
your womb will give birth to a son
destined for the throne of God.

And I told you
that I'm a woman of flesh and blood
and if I'm not joined to a man
the divine lamb cannot be born."

And you said unto me
that nothing is impossible for God
who made the earth and sky,
a man from clay,
and then a woman
from a bone of Adam's rib."

"I said to you,
I am the angel Gabriel
descended from heaven
by the will of God..."
"You did not tell me
they would condemn,

flagillatu e crucifissu;
non mi dicisti
ca l'avissiru chiamatu paganu
e anima dannata.

Io mi scippava i vudedda,
l'appizzava a un chiovu a fétiri:
cu è dda matri
ca parturisci un figghiu
pi cantaricci u martoriu nta naca?

Dda matri
ca parturisci un figghiu
e ci torci u coddu?

Dda matri
beccamorti di so figghiu
ca ci scava a fossa nto lettu
pi trentatrianni?
Rispunni si sì ancilu,
si la tò lingua non è spata,
rispunni!"

Silenziu,
parra u Misia...
Ascutati.
"Donna, non piccari,
non piccari!"

"Peccu p'amuri, figghiu,
peccu pi rimorsu:
io ti scannavu,
io t'appizzavu a cruci:
tò matri a macillara du diavulu!"

Guardati u Misia,
cala a testa scunfittu,

scourge, and crucify him;
You did not say
they would call him a pagan
and a damned soul."

I would have torn my womb out
and hung it on a nail to fester.
Who is that mother
who gives birth to a son
to sing the mourning dirge inside his crib?"

That mother
who gives birth to a son
and twists his neck?

That mother
who's a gravedigger for her son
who digs a grave in his bed
for thirty-three years?
Answer me if you're an angel,
if your tongue is not a sword,
answer me."

Silence,
the Messiah is speaking...
Listen.
"Woman, do not commit a sin!
Do not commit a sin."

"My sin is love, my son,
I'm sinning for remorse.
I slaughtered you,
I nailed you to the cross.
Your mother was a butcher for the devil."

Look at the Messiah,
he lowered his head resigned,

chianci;
supra a vuci di so matri
senti a vuci di giudèi:
crucifigi!
crucifigi!
S'adduna
ca i so paroli d'amuri
i canciaru in dinari
p'accattari e vìnniri.

S'adduna
ca non è l'ura
chi nuàtri aspittamu
dopo vinti seculi;
luttannu ogni ghiornu,
murennu nte carciri,
sparati nte chiazzi.
L'ura c'ogni omu
si spremi u vilenu du cori
e si fa frati o prossimu.

L'ura di vrudicari
i cadàvari di cinniri
di scribi e di farisei
senza testa e senza gammi
ca nàtanu nto sangu di poviri.

U tistamentu u fici,
u grida di mortu!

he is crying;
over his mother's voice
he hears the voices of the Jews:
crucify him,
crucify him!
He realizes
that his words of love
were exchanged for money
to buy and sell."

He realizes
that it is not the hour
we have awaited for
twenty centuries,
struggling every day
dying in prisons
shot in public squares.
The hour that every man
squeezes the poison from his heart
and becomes a brother to his fellow man.

The hour to bury
the ashen cadavers
of scribes and pharisees
without a head and without legs
that swim in the blood of the poor.

He made his testament,
and shouts it from his death.

Lamentu pi Turiddu Carnivali

(Da *Lu trenu di lu suli*)

Ancilu era e non avìa ali
non era santu e miraculi facìa,
ncelu acchianava senza cordi e scali
e senza appidamenti nni scinnìa;
era l'amuri lu sò capitali
e sta ricchizza a tutti la spartìa:
Turiddu Carnivali nnuminatu
e comu Cristu muriu ammazzatu.

Di nicu lu patruzzu un canuscìu,
appi la matri svinturata a latu.
cumpagna a lu duluri e a lu pinìu
e picca pani cu stenti sudatu;
Cristu di ncelu lu binidicíu,
ci dissi: "Figghiu, tu mori ammazzatu;
a Sciara li patruna, armi addannati,
ammazzanu a cu voli libirtati."

Turiddu avìa li jorna cuntati
ma ncuntrava la morti e ci ridìa,
cà vidìa li frati cunnannati
sutta li pedi di la tirannia,
li carni di travagghiu macinati
supra lu cippu a fàrinni tumìa,
e suppurtari non putìa l'abusu
di lu baruni e di lu mafiusu.

Arricugghìu li poviri, amurusu,
li dorminterra, li facci a tridenti,
li manciapicca cu lu ciatu chiusu:
lu tribunali di li pinitenti.
E fici liga di sta carni e pusu
ed arma pi luttari a li putenti
nni ddu paisi esiliatu e scuru

Lament for Turiddu Carnivali

He was an angel and he had no wings,
was not a saint, yet he made miracles.
He rose to heaven without ropes or stairs;
and he climbed down without supports.
Love was the capital that he possessed,
and all this wealth he shared with everyone.
Turiddu Carnivali was his name.
Christ's murder and Turiddu's were the same.

He did not know his father as a child.
He had his star-crossed mother by his side,
as a companion to his suffering and pain,
with little bread earned through hard work and sweat.
From heaven Jesus blessed him and then said:
"My son, you will die by assassination.
Those damnèd souls who own the Sciara land
kill those who take for liberty a stand."

Turiddu's days on earth were numbered, planned,
but often he met death and laughed at it,
because he saw his fellow men condemned,
suffering under the yoke of tyranny.
Their flesh and bodies crushed upon
the butcher block that made mincemeat of them;
because he could no longer tolerate
abuses by the baron and his mafia mate.

Through love, he gathered the unfortunate,
the homeless, the dirt poor, and all the ones
who eat but little bites with bated breath:
and the tribunal of the penitents.
He forged this flesh and wrists into a weapon
to wage a war against the powerful
in that out of the main, exiled, dark site

unni la storia avìa truvatu un muru.

Dissi a lu jurnateri: "Tu sì nnuru,
e la terra è vistuta a pompa magna;
tu la zappi e ci sudi comu un mulu
e sì all'additta siccu na lasagna;
veni la cota ed a corpu sicuru
lu patruni li beni s'aggranfagna
e tu chi fusti ogni matina all'antu
grapi li manu ed arricogghi chiantu.

Fatti curaggiu e non aviri scantu
ca veni jornu e scinni lu Misia,
lu sucialismu cu l'ali di mantu
ca porta pani paci e puisia;
veni si tu lu voi, si tu sì santu,
si sì nnimicu di la tirannia,
s'abbrazzi chista fidi e chista scola
ca duna amuri e l'òmini cunzola.

Lu sucialismu ca la sò parola
pigghia di nterra l'òmini e l'acchiana,
e scurri comu acqua di cannòla
e unni arriva arrifrisca e sana
e dici ca la carni non è sola
e mancu è farina chi si scana:
uguali tutti, travagghiu pi tutti,
tu manci pani si lu sudi e scutti."

Dissi a li jurnateri: "Nta li grutti,
nta li tani durmiti e nta li staddi;
siti comu li surci nte cunnutti,
vi cuntintati di fasoli e taddi;
Ottuviru vi lassa a labbra asciutti
e Giugnu cu li debiti e li caddi,
di l'alivi nn'aviti la ràmagghia
e di la spica la ristuccia e pagghia."

where history met a wall it could not fight.

He told the laborers: "You are stark naked,
the land, however, wears resplendent clothes.
You dig your hoe and like a mule you sweat;
and you stand there much thinner than a rail;
The harvest comes and ever, without fail,
the owner comes and swipes all of the bounty
and you who labored hard from dawn to dusk,
on opening your hands, you see just husk.

Steel yourself with courage, do not fear!
The day is dawning when the Lord will come,
socialism with the mantle wings
that will bring bread, with peace and poetry;
come (if you want it, if you are a saint,
if you're an enemy of tyranny,
if you embrace this faith, this education
that offers love, and gives men consolation.

Socialism is a force that with its words
picks people from the ground and lifts them higher.
It flows free like the water from a fountain,
and where it goes it cools down and it heals;
and says that meat is not sole for your shoes
and that it is not flour you can kneed:
equality for all, and work for all.
You'll eat bread if you sweat and pay the toll.

"You sleep in caverns," he then told
the laborers, "in burrows and in stables;
you are like mice that hide inside a sewer.
You're satisfied with beans and cabbage stumps.
October leaves you with parched lips
and June with callouses and debts;
from olive trees dead leaves are all you get
and straw and lowly chaff instead of wheat.

Dissi: "La terra è di cu la travagghia,
pigghiati li banneri e li zappuna!"
E prima ancora chi spuntassi l'arba
ficiru conchi e scavàru fussuna:
addivintò la terra na tuvagghia,
viva, di carni comu na pirsuna;
e sutta la russìa di li banneri
parsi un giganti ogni jurnateri.

Curreru lesti li carrubbineri
cu li scupetti nmanu e li catini;
Turiddu ci gridò: "Jiti nn'arrèri!
cca non c'è latri, cca non c'è assassini,
ci sunnu cca l'afflitti jurnateri
ca mancu sangu hannu nta li vini:
siddu circati latruna e briganti
nte palazzi i truvati e cu l'amanti."

Lu marascialu fici un passu avanti,
dissi: "La liggi, chistu un lu cunsenti."
Turiddu ci rispusi sull'istanti:
"La vostra è a liggi di li priputenti,
ma c'è una liggi chi non sbagghia e menti
e dici: pani a li panzi vacanti,
robbi a li nudi, acqua a l'assitati
e a cu travagghia anuri e libirtati!"

La mafia priparava scupittati;
sta liggi non garbava a li patruna,
eranu comu li cani arraggiati
cu li denti azziccati nte garruna.
Poviri jurnateri sfurtunati
ca l'aviti di ncoddu a muzzicuna!
Turiddu si guardava di dd'armàli
e stava all'erta si vidìa sipàli.[1]

1. I mafiusi spissu s'ammucciavanu darreri li sipali pi sparari.

He said: "The land belongs to those who sweat,
Pick up the banners and the hoes!"
And even sooner than the break of dawn
they dug out holes and some deep trenches:
the land became a living tablecloth
of flesh and blood just like a person,
and underneath that huge, red colored sea,
each laborer a giant seemed to be.

The police squads arrived, immediately,
with rifles in their hands and many chains.
Turiddu yelled to them: "Do not advance!
These are not thieves, there are no killers here;
only afflicted laborers are here,
with hardly any blood inside their veins:
of thieves and bandits here there are no signs,
find them in rich homes with their concubines."

The marshal in response moved up the line
and said: "The Law does not allow for this,"
Turiddu then replied immediately:
"Yours is the law that bullies understand,
but there's a law that never lies or strays,
that says: give bread to empty stomachs,
clothe the nude, water for those who thirst;
to workers freedom and respect comes first."

The mafia was preparing rifle bursts.
Landowners did not like that law at all,
reacting like a pack of rabid dogs,
sinking their fangs upon the workers' heels.
Poor and unlucky laborers who have
those dogs on your back biting you!
Turiddu was quite wary of those beasts,
and kept his eyes on hedges as he passed.[1]

1. Mafia killers often hid behind hedges to shoot.

Na sira turnò dintra senza ali
l'occhi luntanu e lu pinzeri puru:
"Mancia figghiu miu, cori liali ..."
ma chiù lu guarda, chiù lu vidi scuru:
"Figghiu," ci dissi, "chi ti senti mali?"
e cu la menti fici lu scunciuru.
"Matri," dissi Turiddu e la guardò,
"bonu mi sentu"; e la testa calò.

"Figghiu," ci dissi, "cu t'amminazzò?
sugnu tò matri non m'ammucciari nenti."
Matri, vinni lu jornu," e suspirò;
"A Cristu l'ammazzaru e fu nnuccenti!"
"Figghiu, lu cori miu assincupò,
mi ci azzicasti tri spati puncenti!"
Genti ca siti cca, fàciti vuci:
la matri si lu vitti mortu ncruci.

Sidici maggiu, l'arba ncelu luci,
e lu casteddu àutu di Sciara
taliàva lu mari chi straluci
comu n'artàru supra di na vara;
e fra mari e casteddu una gran cruci
si vitti dda matina all'aria chiara,
sutta la cruci un mortu, e cu l'aceddi
lu chiantu ruttu di li puvireddi.

Gridava, figghiu pi strati e vaneddi
la strangusciata matri chi currza
pi la trazzera a stramazzamareddi:
un fasciu di sarmenti chi svampia
dintra d'un furnu e ventu a li spurteddi:
"Curriti tutti a chiànciri cu mia!
Puvireddi, nisciti di li tani,
morsi ammazzatu pi lu vostru pani!"

"Carrubbineri, si sì cristianu,

One night he went back home glum and depressed.
His eyes stared far away and his thoughts too;
"Please eat, my son, my loyal, faithful heart..."
But watching him she knew he was distraught.
"My son," she asked, "Do you feel sick? What's wrong?"
But in her mind, she kept her fingers crossed.
He looked his mother in the eyes and said:
"I feel all right," and lowered then his head.

"My son, did someone threaten you?" she said
"I am your mother, don't hide anything ..."
"Mother, my day has come," and then he sighed;
"They murdered Christ, and he was innocent."
"My son, my heart is bursting from the pain!
You're driving three sharp swords into my brain!"
You people standing here, shout for this loss!
His mother saw her son dead on the cross.

It is now May sixteen, the dawn's bright gloss
on Sciara's castle looked down from its height,
gazing upon the sea that was aglitter,
just like an altar carried on a bier.
Between the castle and the sea, a cross
was seen that morning in the vibrant air.
Under the cross a dead man. With the birds'
the broken sobbing of the poor was heard.

The mother, screaming for her son, just whirred
through streets and alleyways in desperation,
running haphazardly at breakneck speed:
she was a bunch of dry vine shoots aflame
inside an oven fed by driving wind:
"Come running all and weep along with me,
poor folk, out of your lairs! He is now dead!
and he was murdered just to give you bread.

"Policeman, if humanity's not dead

non mi tuccari, levati di ddocu:
non vidi ca su torci li me manu
e addumu comu pruvuli a lu focu:
chistu è me figghiu, vattinni luntanu,
quantu lu chiànciu e lu duluri sfogu,
quantu ci sciogghiu dda palumma bianca
c'havi dintra lu pettu a manu manca.

Carrubbineri, si sì cristianu
e non hai lu cori di Cainu,
fammi ncugnari ca ci levu chianu
sta petra c'havi misa pi cuscinu;
sutta la facci ci mettu sti manu
supra lu pettu lu cori vicinu,
e cu lu chiantu li chiaj ci sanu
prima c'agghiorna dumani matinu.

Prima c'agghiorna trovu l'assassinu
e ci scippu lu cori cu sti manu,
lu portu strascinannu a lu parrinu:
sunati li campani, sagristanu!
Me figghiu avìa lu sangu d'oru finu
e chistu di pisciazza di pantanu,
chiamaticci na tigri pi bicchinu
la fossa ci la scavu cu sti manu.

Figghiu, chi dicu? La testa mi sguazza ...
Oh, si non fussi pi la fidi mia!
Lu sucialismu chi grapi li vrazza
e mi duna la spiranza e la valìa;
mi lu nzignasti e mi tinevi mbrazza
ed io supra li manu ti chiancìa,
tu m'asciucavi cu lu muccaturi
io mi sintìa mòriri d'amuri.

Tu mi parravi comu un cunfissuri
io ti parrava comu pinitenti;

in you, don't touch me, move away from there;
do you not see that my hands are ablaze,
and I am burning like dust in the fire?
This is my son, stay far away from him,
so I may weep for him and vent my grief;
so I may liberate the snow-white dove
he harbored on the left side as pure love.

"Policeman, if you are a Christian,
and do not have a heart like Cain,
allow me to get close so I can move
the rock that serves as pillow for his head
my hands I will place underneath his face,
and put my heart upon his chest right close,
so with my tears I'll heal his wounds and sorrow
before the break of dawn arrives tomorrow.

I'll find the killer before dawn tomorrow,
and with these hands I will tear out his heart,
I'll drag him to the priest along the streets.
You, sacristan, go ring all the church bells!
My son had blood of fine-spun gold,
and this one had marsh urine in his veins.
As undertaker for a tiger send
and I will dig his grave with my bare hands.

Son, what do I say? I'm at my wits' end…
Oh if it were not for my burning faith!
Our socialism that opens up my arms
and gives me hope and strength to cope.
You taught me as you held me in your arms
and as I wept upon your patient hands,
your handkerchief wiped down tears from my face.
I felt quite overcome with love and grace.

You talked to me as a confessor does;
I talked to you as though I were a sinner.

ora disfatta pi tantu duluri
ci dugnu vuci a li cumannamenti:
vogghiu muriri du tò stissu amuri,
vogghiu muriri cu sti sintimenti.
Figghiu, ti l'arrubbavu la bannera,
matri ti sugnu e cumpagna sincera!

Distraught as I am for my pain and woes,
I now make known my life's commandments:
I want to die from the same love you had,
I want to die with the same sentiments.
My son, your banner as my own I claim;
mother and a true sister's now my aim.

Lu trenu di lu suli

(Da *Lu trenu di lu suli*)

Turi Scordu, surfararu,
abitanti a Mazzarinu;
cu lu Trenu di lu suli
s'avvintura a lu distinu.

Chi faceva a Mazzarinu
si travagghiu nun ci nn'era?
fici sciopiru na vota
e lu misiru ngalera.

Una tana la sò casa,
quattru ossa la muggheri;
e la fami lu circava
cu li carti di l'usceri.

Setti figghi e la muggheri,
ottu vucchi ed ottu panzi,
e lu cori un camiuni
carricatu di dugghianzi.

Nni lu Belgiu, nveci,
ora travagghiava jornu e notti;
a la mogghi ci scriveva:
nun manciati favi cotti.

Cu li sordi chi ricivi
compra roba e li linzola,
e li scarpi pi li figghi
pi putiri jri a scola.

Li mineri di lu Belgiu,
li mineri di carbuni:
sunnu niri niri niri
comu sangu di draguni.

The Train of the Sun

Turi Scordu, sulfur miner,
a Mazzarinu resident,
took the train of the sun:
tempting fate was his intent.

Could he stay in Mazzarino
if there was no work to find?
He once joined a workers strike
and in prison was confined.

A poor hovel was his home,
skin and bones defined his wife;
hunger kept pursuing him
through a bill collector's strife.

Seven children and a wife,
and eight bellies with eight mouths,
and his heart a camion rife
with calamities and doubts.

But in Belgium now instead
he was working day and night;
"Don't eat fava beans!" he said
to his wife when he would write.

With the money you receive
buy bedsheets and clothes with wool
and good shoes for all the kids
so they can all go to school.

In the mining towns of Belgium
you dig coal, through sweat and mud,
that is blacker than the night,
like the black of dragon's blood.

Turi Scordu, un pezzu d'omu,
a la sira dormi sulu;
ntra lu lettu a pedi fora
smaniava comu un mulu.

Cu li fimmini ntintava;
ma essennu analfabeta,
nun aveva pi ncantarli
li paroli di pueta.

E faceva pinitenza
Turi Scordu nni lu Belgiu:
senza tònaca e né mitra
ci pareva un sacrilegiu.

Certi voti lu pinseri
lu purtava ntra la tana,
e lu cori ci sunava
a martoriu la campana.

Ca si c'era la minestra
di patati e di fasoli,
nni dda tana c'era festa
pi la mogghi e li figghioli.

Comu arvulu scippatu
senza radichi e né fogghi,
si sinteva Turi Scordu
quannu penza figghi e mogghi.

Doppu un annu di patiri
finalmenti si dicisi:
«Mogghi mia, pigghia la roba,
venitinni a stu paisi».

E parteru matri e figghi,
salutaru Mazzarinu;

Turi Scordu, a big man,
whose feet hung outside the bed,
slept alone just like a mule,
his libido though not fed.

He would try his luck with women,
but as an illiterate,
he did not possess the words
to enchant a good playmate.

Turi Scordu there in Belgium
was a penitent, on edge,
without tunic or a miter
it all seemed a sacrilege.

Often times his mind would go
to the lair where he did dwell,
in his heart he then could hear
somber sounds of mourning bells.

If there was potato soup
or bean soup inside that lair,
for the wife and for the kids
there was feasting in the air.

Like a tree that's been dug up,
Turi Scordu lived a life,
without roots and without leaves,
when he thought of kids and wife.

After suffering a year,
he decided: "My dear wife,
pack your things immediately.
Here we'll have a better life."

So the mother and the children
from their hometown went away.

li parenti pi d'appressu
ci facevanu fistinu.

Na valiggia di cartuni
cu la corda pi traversu;
nni lu pettu lu nutricu
chi sucava a tempu persu.

La cuvata cu la ciocca
quannu fu supra lu trenu,
nun sapeva s'era ncelu...
si tuccava lu tirrenu.

Lu paisi di luntanu
ora acchiana e ora scinni;
e lu trenu ca vulava
senza ali e senza pinni.

Ogni tantu si firmava
pi nfurnari passaggeri:
emigranti surfarara,
figghi, patri e li muggheri.

Patri e matri si prisentanu,
li fa amici la svintura:
l'emigranti na famigghia
fannu dintra la vittura.

«Lu me nomu? Rosa Scordu».
«Lu paisi? Mazzarinu».
«Unni jiti ?». «Unni jiamu?
Unni voli lu distinu!».

Quantu cosi si cuntaru!
ca li poviri, si sapi,
hannu guai a miliuna:
muzzicati di li lapi!

All their relatives applauded
cheered them on along the way.

One suitcase made of cardboard,
with a rope tied scantily
and an infant at her breast
who was sucking leisurely.

When the hen and all her chicks
were inside the moving train,
they knew not if up in heaven,
or on earth the train remained.

Their own town from far away
moved straight up and then moved down,
and the train was flying high,
without wings and without downs.

The train stopped once in a while,
stuffing passengers inside:
emigrating sulfur miners,
fathers, mothers, kids in stride.

Fathers, mothers now made friends,
they were bound by their calamity:
all those emigrants inside
could be thought as one big family.

"What's my name?" "Rosa Scordu,"
"City?" "Mazzarinu is my town"
"Destination?" "Where fate wants.
Fate on this will wear the crown."

How many things they shared
with each other, for the poor,
as we know, are stung by bees,
and they have of woes galore.

Quannu vinni la nuttata
doppu Villa San Giuvanni
una radiu tascabili
addiverti nichi e granni.

Tutti sentinu la radiu,
l'havi nmanu n'emigranti;
li carusi un hannu sonnu,
fannu l'occhi granni tanti.

Rosa Scordu ascuta e penza,
cu lu sapi chi va a trova...
n'àtra genti e nazioni,
una storia tutta nova.

E si strinci pi difisa
lu nutricu nsunnacchiatu
mentri l'occhi teni ncoddu
di li figghi a lu sò latu.

E la radiu tascabili
sona musica di ballu;
un discursu di ministru;
un minutu d'intervallu.

Poi detti li nutizii,
era quasi menzannotti:
sunnu l'ultimi nutizii
li nutizii di la notti.

La radio trasmette: «Ultime notizie della notte. Una grave sciagura si è verificata in Belgio nel distretto min:erario di Charleroi. Per cause non ancora note una esplosione ha sconvolto uno dei livelli della miniera di Marcinelle. Il numero delle vittime è assai elevato».

Ci fu un lampu di spaventu

After Villa San Giovanni,
with the dark of night outside,
someone with a little radio
cheer to young and old supplied.

They all listened to the radio
that the emigrant possessed.
All the children were not sleepy
and they listened much impressed.

Rosa Scordu heard and thought
about what she might find there…
A new people, a new country:
a new life hung in the air.

And she hugged her infant close
who was tired, sleepy-eyed,
while she carefully watched over
all the others by her side.

The small radio broadcast
dancing music for some time,
then a long speech by a minister,
interrupted by a chime.

The news program then began:
the time was close to midnight.
The small radio announced
the last newscast of the night.

Radio broadcast: "A serious accident has occurred in Belgium in the mining district of Charleroi. For causes not yet known an explosion rocked one of the levels of the mine of Marcinelle. The number of victims is very high."

Everybody's breath just froze,

chi siccò lu ciatu a tutti;
Rosa Scordu sbarra l'occhi,
focu e lacrimi s'agghiutti.

La radio continua a trasmettere: «I primi cadaveri riportati alla superficie dalle squadre di soccorso appartengono a nostri connazionali emigrati dalla Sicilia. Ecco il primo elenco delle vittime. Natale Fatta, di Riesi provincia di Caltanissetta, Francesco Tilotta, di Villarosa provincia di Enna Alfio Calabrò, di Agrigento Salvatore Scordu... ».

Un trimotu: «Me maritu!
me maritu!» grida e chianci,
e li vuci sangu e focu
dintra l'occhi comu lanci.

Cu na menti e centu vucchi,
addumata comu torcia,
si lamenta e l'ugna affunna
ntra li carni e si li scorcia.

L'àutra manu strinci e ammacca
lu nutricu stramurtutu,
ca si torci mentri chianci
affucatu e senza aiutu.

E li figghi? cu capisci,
cu capisci e cu un capisci,
annigati nmenzu a l'unni
di ddu mari senza pisci.

Rosa Scordu, svinturata,
nun è fimmina e né matri,
e li figghi sunnu orfani
di la matri e di lu patri.

Misi attornu l'emigranti

stricken by a burst of fear;
Rosa Scordu with wide eyes
swallowed fire with her tears.

The radio continued: "The bodies recovered by the first responders so far are of Sicilian emigrants. The first list of the victims follows: Natale Fatta from Riesi, province of Caltanissetta, Francesco Tilotta from Villarosa, provincia di Enna, Alfio Calabrò, from Agrigento, Salvatore Scordu ..."

An earthquake: "My husband, Oh!"
Rosa Scordu screams and cries,
and her voice of blood and fire,
are like lances in her eyes.

With one mind and hundred mouths
that is lit just like a flame,
she her claws sinks in her flesh,
and her body starts to maim.

With the other hand she grabs
the poor infant, who's afraid,
who is squirming as it cries,
out of breath and without aid.

And the other children? Some
understand, others can't see,
or hear, drowning in the waves,
in that awesome, barren sea.

Rosa Scordu, poor, distraught,
neither woman is nor mother
and her children are now orphans
both of father and the mother.

All the emigrants around

ca nun sannu zoccu fari;
sunnu puru nmenzu a l'unni:
strascinati di ddu mari.

Va lu trenu nni la notti,
chi nuttata longa e scura:
non ci fu lu funirali,
è na fossa la vittura.

Turi Scordu a la finestra,
a lu vitru mpiccicatu,
senza occhi, senza vucca:
è un schelitru abbruciatu.

L'arba vinni senza lustru,
Turi Scordu ddà ristava:
Rosa Scordu lu strinceva
nni li vrazza, e s'abbruciava.

don't know if they could do more.
They too are amidst those waves
that sweep them out from the shore.

The train rolled along the tracks.
Oh what long and gloomy night!
While there was no funeral,
that train coach was a grave site.

Turi Scordu at the window,
was stuck on the window glass,
without eyes and without mouth,
he looked like a scorched carcass.

Then dawn came without much light,
Turi Scordu did transpire;
Rosa Scordu held him tight,
in her arms and was on fire.

A Sicilia avi un patruni

A Sicilia avi un patruni
un patruni sempri uguali
ca la teni misa ncruci
e ci canta u funirali.

La Sicilia avi un guvernu
un guvernu talianu
cu la furca a lu capizzu
e la corda 'nta li manu

La Sicilia avi na patria
chi la strinci 'nta li vrazza
ma 'nzammai dumanna pani
finci dallu e ccà n'ammazza.

La Sicilia è spupulata
un desertu ogni paisi
vecchi e cani 'nta li strati
picciriddi scavusi misi.

Li picciotti sunnu fora
ca li vrazza l'hannu sani
ma lu patri talianu
si vinnìu npezzu di pani

La Sicilia è addummisciuta
comu un sonnu di li morti
e s'aspetta mentri dormi
chi canciassi la so' sorti.

Ma la sorti unn'è ostia,
unn'è grazia di li santi.
Si cunquista cu la forza
'nta li chiazzi e si va avanti,

Sicily Has a Master

Sicily has a master.
It is ever the same scourge
that keeps it upon the cross
and then chants a deadly dirge.

Sicily has a government
ruled by Italians
with a noose close by the pillow
and a rope held in its hands.

Sicily has a motherland
that holds it with arms widespread,
but if it should ask for bread
She pretends to give it but
she will give it death instead.

Sicily is now deserted,
no more people can it lose!
In the streets old people, dogs,
and poor children with no shoes.

The young men have left the island.
They possess strong arms and hands,
but they were sold for two cents
by the fathers of the land.

Sicily is fast asleep
and Sicilians all await,
in their death-like prolonged sleep,
a good change in their harsh fate.

But our fate is not a host,
it is not a saintly grace.
You must win it with your might
in the streets and every place.

si cunquista cu la forza
'nta li chiazzi e si va avanti.

You must win it with your might
in the streets, advance and fight.

Purtedda dâ Ginestra

(Da *Le pietre nere*)

Nta lu chianu dâ Purtedda
chiusa a 'n menzu a ddu' muntagni
c'è 'na petra supra l'erba
pi ricordu a li compagni.

A l'addritta nni 'sta petra
a lu tempu di li Fasci [1]
un apostulu parrava
di lu beni pi cu nasci.

E di tannu finu a ora
a Purtedda dâ Ginestra
quannu veni 'u primu maggiu
'i cumpagni fannu festa...

E Giulianu lu sapìa
ch'era 'a festa di li poviri,
'Na jurnata tuttasuli
doppu tantu tempu a chiòviri

Cu ballava, cu cantava,
cu accurdava li canzuni
E li tavuli cunzati
di nuciddi e di turrùni!

Zitu e zita cu la manu
nni la manu cu li caddi;
zitu e zita chi caminanu
e si stricanu li spaddi.

Ogni asta di bannera,
era zappa, vrazza e manu.

1 Si riferisce Nicola Barbato, presidente dei Fasci dei lavoratori siciliani (1892-1894).

Purtedda dâ Ginestra

In the plain of the Purtedda,
bound by mountains on each side,
there's a stone upon the grass
that our comrades dignified.

Standing there upon that stone
when the farmers rose in mass [1]
an apostle spoke of things
that all mankind should possess.

From that time until today
when it is the first of May
at Purtedda dâ Ginestra
our comrades all come to play.

And Giuliano knew that this
was a feast day for the poor.
It was sunny on that day,
after rain for long had poured.

Some were dancing, others sang,
harmonizing all the tunes;
hazel nuts and nougat candy
were on tables richly strewn.

There were couples holding hands;
smooth and calloused hands were those
of betrothed walking slowly,
with their shoulders rubbing close.

Ev'ry pole that raised a flag
was a hoe, with arms and feet,

1 The poet is referring to Nicola Barbato, president of the Union of Sicilian workers (1892-1894).

era terra siminata,
era furnu, furnu e granu.

La spiranza d'un dumani
chi fa 'u munnu 'na famigghia
la vidèvunu vicinu
e cuntavunu li migghia.

L'uraturi di ddu jornu
jera Japicu Schirò,
dissi: «Viva 'u primu maggiu»,
e la lingua ci siccò.

Di lu munti 'i la Pizzuta
ch'è l'artura cchiù vicina
Giulianu e la so banna
scatinô 'a carneficina.

A tappitu e a vintagghiu,
mitragghiavunu la genti
comu fauci chi metinu
cu lu vampi nni li denti,

Scappa a fudda, spavintata,
nni lu chianu e grida, aiutu!
e currennu jsa i vrazza
pi difisa comu scutu.

E li matri cu lu ciatu,
cu lu ciatu – senza ciatu:
– Figghiu miu, corpu e vrazza
comu ghiommaru aggruppatu!

Pi discriviri la scena
ci vurrissi un rumanzeri:
sta chitarra un sapi chiànciri,
mmalidittu stu misteri!

it was land that had been seeded,
it was oven, bread, and wheat.

The hope for a future day
when the world a family
would become was before them
at a distance they could see.

Schirò Jacopo, the speaker,
said one sentence on that day:
and his tongue dried in his mouth:
"Long life to the First of May!"

From the mountain La Pizzuta,
on the high ground, near the crest,
Giuliano and his gang
then unleashed their slaughter fest.

Strafing randomly across the plain,
—those poor folks had no retreat—,
their machine guns sprayed the people.
'Twas like scythes that harvest wheat.

Some began to run in terror,
others fled across the field,
others threw their arms in air,
trying to use them as a shield.

And the mothers out of breath
with their breath and breathlessly,
– Oh my son, your arms and body
are a knot tied dreadfully.

To describe this scenery
you must be a novelist,
this guitar just cannot weep,
no one else can I enlist.

Doppu un quartu di ddu 'nfernu,
(vita, morti e passioni,)
'i briganti si nni jeru
senza cchiù munizioni,

Supra i petri e supra u sangu
ammazzati a tradimentu
arristaru vinti poviri
e firuti chiù di centu.

Supra i petri e nmenzu u sangu
figghi e matri addinucchiati
cu li lacrimi li facci
ci lavavanu a vasati.

Epifania Barbato
a lu figghiu mortu nterra
ci dicìa: "A li poviri,
puru cca ci fannu guerra!"

Margherita, la Clisceri,
ch'era dda cu cincu figghi
arristò ammazzata nterra,
e nno ventri u sestu figghiu.

Cu ddu jornu fu a Purtedda,
cu ci va doppu tant'anni,
vidi i morti caminari
caminari senza gammi.

Vivi ancora, ancora vivi;
e na vuci ncelu e nterra,
e na vuci ncelu e nterra:
oh giustizia, quannu arrivi?!

Fifteen minutes of that hell,
(passions, life and brutal death),
with no bullets in their guns,
all the bandits simply left.

Upon stones, in pools of blood,
they left twenty people dead,
and a hundred wounded more,
who were hurt in that bloodshed.

On the stones and in the blood
sons and mothers on their knees,
washed the faces of the dead
with their kisses and their tears.

Epifania Barbatu
told her dead son on the floor:
"Even here they now wage war
on the helpless and the poor!"

Margarita La Glisceri
was there with her kids, all five,
all were shot with the sixth one
she had in her womb alive.

If you were at the Purtedda
and return there after long,
you will see the murdered people
without legs who walk along.

They're still living, still alive,
and you will then hear a voice,
in the sky and on the earth:
Justice, when will you arrive?!

Ncuntravu u Signuri

(Da *Io faccio il poeta*)

Ncuntravu u Signuri pa strata
e ci dissi:
nun t'affrunti a caminari scausu?

Era stancu.
L'ossa arrusicati da càmula,
a tonaca sfardata
a vucca sicca
e circava acqua.

Facìa pietati a vidillu.
Ma pinzannu a chiddu chi nni fici
pu piaciri di mittirinni o munnu
e vidirinni arrubbari, odiari, assicutari i danari
e gudiri du mali di l'autri,
vi dicu a virità:
non mi spuntò na lacrima.

E facìa mprissioni
un picciottu di trentatrianni
beddu,
gàvutu,
ussutu,
e l'occhi di ova di palumma
figghiati nta pagghia.

Facìa mprissioni
da taliatura d'omu
ca traseva nto cori
cu ventu du ciatu,
nto cori commu lingua d'agneddu
e crapicchi di matri.

Ma pinzannu chiddu chi ni feci

I Encountered the Lord

I encountered the Lord in the street
and said to him:
have you no shame, walking barefoot like that?

He was exhausted.
His bones gnawed by worms,
his tunic torn,
his mouth bone dry,
he was looking for water.

It grieved me to see him like that.
But thinking of what he'd done for us
for the pleasure of giving us life
and watch us steal and hate, chase after gold,
rejoicing for the woes of others,
I tell you the truth,
I did not shed a tear.

And he was quite remarkable:
a man thirty-three years of age
handsome,
tall,
bony,
with eyes shaped like dove's eggs
laid out on straw.

It was quite striking
the way he looked at you
that pierced right through your heart
with the gentleness of a breath,
into the heart like a lamb's tongue
and a mother's nipples.

But thinking of what he did for us

pu piaciri di vidirinni
scippari l'occhi l'unu cu l'autru,
scurciari l'unu cu l'autru, ammazzarinni,
e chiantari banneri di vittoria
nte panzi di morti,
vi dicu a virità:
non mi spuntò una lacrima.

Ci dissi sulu:
megghiu si non nascevi,
non scinnevi nterra
e non murivi nta cruci.

Nuàtri fussimu nenti,
nè pampini nè ciuri
e mancu carni punciuta di l'api
e manciata di vermi.

Fussimu nenti,
negghi senza timpesta
e senza trona e lampi nto cielu
e tirrimoto nterra...
nenti.

Era stancu,
mi taliava e chiancìa
comu unu nnuccenti
ch'acchiana o patibulu.

for the pleasure of seeing us
tear out each other's eyes,
stripping each other's skin, murdering,
and raising banners of victory
on the bellies of the dead,
I tell you the truth,
I did not shed a tear.

I only said to him:
better if you had not been born,
not coming down to earth,
and dying on the cross.

Nothing we would have been,
neither leaves nor flowers,
not even flesh stung by the bees
and eaten by foul worms.

We would be nothing,
fogs without a storm,
without thunder and lightning in the sky,
and without earthquakes on land...
nothing.

He was exhausted,
he looked at me and he kept crying
like a guiltless man
climbing onto the gallows.

I petri nivuri

(Da *Pietre nere*)

A Roberto Roversi
ai suoi anni lunghi ed ai miei corti

Sugnu cca
sulu
stanotti
a scriviri e pinzari
ca i ricordi, i ricordi,
na petra oggi e nàutra dumani
addiventanu muntagni
e nni purtamu ncoddu sinu a morti ...
chi morti.

A pinzari
ca i petri
sunnu nichi e grossi,
nivuri e bianchi,
—chiù nivuri ca bianchi—;
e chi l'omini
(io)
distinati pi natura
a scavari nna mimoria,
n'affannamu a circari
i petri nivuri
c'hannu i chiaj aperti,
sempri aperti,
e i vavareddi vagnati.

E diri
ca sunnu i petri
i petri bianchi
c'adornanu i muntagni
e spicchìanu l'arba d'ogni matinu;
iddi nn'ajsanu dinterra
quannu i furturi nn'annorbanu
e nni sbàttinu a facci abbuccuni.

Black Stones

To Roberto Rversi
to his long years and my short ones

I am here
alone
tonight
to write and think
that memories, the memories,
one stone today, another one tomorrow,
grow into mountains
and on our backs we bear them till we die…
with the dead.

To think
that stones
are small and big,
black and white,
—more black than white—;
and that men
(I)
destined by nature
to dig in memory,
we struggle to find
the black stones
that have open sores,
always open,
and humid pupils.

And say
that it's those stones
the white ones
that adorn the mountains
and make dawn glitter every morning;
they are the ones that raise us from the ground
when storms are blinding us
and throw our faces on the floor.

L'omini u sannu, penzu,
u sannu; e senza vulillu
scordanu i petri bianchi
chi cantanu a vita
e mai i petri nivuri
chi ripetinu u misireri:
l'amanu chiù assai.

I matri,
i matri fannu u stissu:
mettinu nn'artàru
i figghi tinti
ca i carricanu di peni
e non aduranu i boni
ca i cunsulanu
e ci asciucanu i lacrimi.

Nni ricordu una di sti matri:
una tutta focu e chiantu
affirrata a gaggia da Curti d'Assisi
—io era picciriddu—,
ca trasìa e niscìa a testa da nfirriata
e vasava e rivasava
u figghiu assassinu,
du voti assassinu,
cunnannatu a vita.

U vasava; u vasava
e non taliava
a colpu d'occhiu sparatu
l'àutru figghiu, cristianu,
nna gaggia
assoltu e nnuccenti.

M'attuppassi l'occhi
ora ca la ricordu
pi non vidilla, straziata,

Men know this, I think,
they know it; and without wanting to
they forget the white stones
that sing life
and never the black stones
that chant the *miserere*:
they love them more.

Mothers,
mothers do the same thing:
they place upon the altar
the evil sons
who burdened them with sorrows
and do not love the good ones
who comfort them,
who dry their tears.

I remember one of these mothers:
full of fire and of tears,
stuck to the bars of the defendants' cage
inside the Courtroom.
—I was a child then—,
who stuck her head through the bars
and kissed over and over
the son who was a murderer, twice,
condemned to life imprisonment.

She kissed him, repeatedly,
and did not look
at the other son, a Christian,
right there inside the cage,
found not guilty,
innocent.

I feel like covering my eyes
now that I remember her
just not to see her,

davanti a gaggia
tràsiri e nesciri a testa
e manciarisi u ferru a muzzicuna.
M'attuppassi l'occhi
pi non vidiri l' assassinu,
du voti assassinu:
iddu!
chiànciri nna gaggia
mentri tutti u talianu.

Du voti assassinu;
iddu, du voti ...
io quantu voti assassinu?!

Nno Piavi sugnu,
avanzu, sparu, ammazzu:

nno Piavi sugnu!
All'arma bianca cummattu
panzi sbudeddu
morti scarpisu, morti!

E tutti comu mia
armali e cristiani
nnimici e taliani
arditi e spavintati
sarvaggi e vattiati
nno nfernu e nparadisu
nn'artàru e nfurca misi:
tutti comu mia,
assassini comu mia! ...

Vivu sugnu,
tremu ancora:
mi parìa veru.

I petri nivuri. *7 maggio 1981*

before that cage, distraught,
sticking her head between the bars,
in and out,
gnawing at the iron with her teeth.
I feel like covering my eyes
not to see the murderer,
twice a murderer:
crying inside the cage
while everybody watched him.

Twice a murderer
he was, two times…
How many times a murderer am I?!

I'm at the Piave River,
advancing, shooting, killing:

I'm at the Piave River
I'm fighting with a bayonet
I'm disemboweling men
I'm stepping over them

and all like me
animals and people
enemies and Italians
daring and cowardly
infidels and baptized
in hell and paradise,
on altars and on gallows placed:
all of them like me!...
all murderers like me!...

I am alive,
I am still shaking:
It seemed real.

The black stones. *May 7, 1981*

Sillabariu d'amuri

(Da *Pietre nere*)

Stanotti
mentri scrivu
è comu si stassi pi mòriri
e mi cunfissassi
cu mia stissu
pi sippillirimi nni sti carti.

È un tistamentu
chi lassu a l'omini d'oggi
c'arrancanu o scuru
e cu l'amuri ncruci
nno catalettu di l' occhi.

Non è a vicchiaia chi mi supranìa
e mancu a morti chi m'assicuta
chi mi custrinci a fallu:
si fussi idda
—fa parti da vita
si spàrtinu u sonnu
sunnu l'arba e u tramuntu—
l'aspittassi a testa a cursa.

Non è a morti:
è l'allavancu di me sònnira
di pueta pupulari
chi davanu meli
e sucavanu feli
nno cori di l'omini
sudati na muntata
chi di cima ncima
grapìa celi novi.

È un tradimentu,
s'è veru

Love Sillabary

While I write
tonight
it's like I am about to die
and am confessing
with myself
burying myself in these papers.

It is a testament
I leave to men today
who struggle in the dark
and with love on a cross
in the death bed of the eyes.

It's not old age that's lording over me
and not even death pursuing me.
that forces me to do this:
if that were death
—she is part of life
they share their sleep
they are sunrise and sunset—
I'd be the first on line to wait.

It is not death:
it is the crashing of my dreams
as a popular poet
that promised honey
and sucked bitterness
in the hearts of men
sweating as they climbed
a mountain that opened
new skies from every peak.

It's a betrayal,
if it's true

ca a storia a fannu l'omini
e non u casu e a furtuna
e né a grazia calata du celu.
Non li canusciu chiù l'omini:
spirdi assicutati sunnu,
machini parlanti;
pupi di negghia sunnu:
pèrsiru u sangu!

Pèrsiru a vuci
a ntisa
l'occhi pi ncantari,
i manu e i vrazza
pi strinciri e vasari.

Non hannu nenti di spàrtiri.
Non hannu paroli midicati
pi sanari i chjai,
paroli di puisia
pi risuscitari i morti,
paroli d'amuri
pi siminari amuri.

Petri simìnanu,
petri:
recitanu a litania du sonnu
e u lamentu da morti.

Chi notti! ...
addivintò na fossa la me casa:
e tu,
tu, viva nno ritrattu o muru,
— nurrizza mia, povira,
e matri di setti figghi
ca ti turcevi i minni p'addattarimi —
pirdunami
si non haiu animu di ringraziariti

that history is made by men
and not by chance or luck
nor by grace sent from heaven.
I don't know men any more,
they are fleeing ghosts,
talking machines,
puppets made of fog:
they lost their blood!

They lost their voices
their hearing
their seductive eyes'
their hands and arms
to hug and kiss.

They have nothing to share;
they have no words that heal
to cure the wounds,
words of poetry
to resurrect the dead,
words of love
to propagate love.

The sow stones:
stones:
they recite the litany of sleep
and the lament of death.

What a night!
My home has now become a grave:
and you,
you, there alive in the portrait on the wall,
—my poor nursemaid,
mother of seven children
who squeezed your breasts to give me milk—
forgive me
if I don't have the heart to thank you

e di vasari i to manu
ca mi nzignaru a fàrimi
u signu da cruci.

Pirdunami:
u latti chi mi dasti
si fici sangu nvilinatu,
feti nivuru,
carni marciuta
e cori macillatu.

Arripetimi
comu sempri
u to sillabariu d'amuri.

and kiss your hands
that taught me how to make
the sign of the cross.

Forgive me:
the milk you gave to me
has turned to poisoned blood,
black stench,
rotting flesh
and a slaughtered heart.

Repeat for me
as always
your love sillabary.

A natura è facciola

(Da *Pietre nere*)

E semu cca io e vuàtri
a taliarinni nni l' occhi
nna facci
pi sapiri cu semu
cu siti
e chi vinnimu a fari nno munnu
si nascemu pi mòriri:
ci aviti mai pinzatu? ...

Io sì
ora ca sugnu di cògghiri,
e basta un ciusciu d'aria
pi spiccicarimi da rama.

L'anni
a passi curti
mi ficiru scola
nne vanchi du tempu
e mi nzignaru a capiri
a lingua chi parranu
—cu a vuci e senza vuci—
tutti i cosi criati da natura.
E si talìu u mari
e c'è ventu e timpesta
sentu u so gridu rabbiusu
— cu a scuma a vucca —
isari l'unni e sbattilli nne scogghi.

E s'è di nvernu e trunìa
e l'acqua chiovi a diluviu
viu l'arbuli lacrimiari
ed arrunchiari i spaddi scantati.

Comu nuàtri, l'arbuli,

Nature is Two-Faced

And you and I are here
looking into each other's eyes
into our faces
to learn who we are
who you are
and what we came to do on earth
if we were born to die.
Have you ever pondered this?...

I have
now that I'm near the harvest time,
and that a breath of air
is enough to tear me off the branch.

The years
with their slow gait
have instructed me
on the school bench of time
and taught me to understand
the language that is spoken
—with a voice and without voice—
by all things nature has created.
And if I look at the sea
and there is wind and storm
I hear its angry howl
—with the foam or without foam—
churning waves and crashing them on the rocks.

And if it's winter and there's thunder
and water rains in buckets,
I see the trees tearing and gathering
themselves inside their barks, afraid.

The trees, just like ourselves,

quannu ci siccanu i vini
e restanu ossa di lignu additta
penzanu a morti;
e mmalidicinu u suli e a luna
a notti e u jornu
ca fannu lustru e scuru
e non mòrinu mai.

A natura è facciola:
l'arburi morinu abbruciati
e non li chianci nuddu;
dettiru ciuri e frutti
friscu e ummira
e foru naca e nidu a l'aceddi.

È facciola: nuàtri, un muremu,
biatu cu ci cridi e spera
d'attruvari ncelu u patri
a matri
i figghi
chi vrazza aperti
e l'occhi a via c'aspettanu.

D'attruvari na figghia
picciridda
cu vistitinu biancu
e i ciuri nno pettu
comu a vittimu nna cascia
l'urtima vota.

Chi strata longa ...
di nterra ncelu;
e non putemu diri
non la vogghiu fari,
e mancu
vogghiu iri a vidiri u paisi
l'amici

when their veins dry up,
remaining upright like wooden bones,
will think of death;
and curse the sun and moon
night and day
creating light and darkness
and never die.

Nature is two-faced:
the trees die burned to death
and no one mourns for them;
they produced fruits and flowers,
they gave us coolness, shade,
and nests, cradles for birds.

It's two-faced: we, we don't die,
blessed are those who believe and hope
to find in heaven their father,
their mother,
their children,
with their arms open
and with eyes toward the road, waiting;

to find a daughter
as a child
with her pretty white dress
with a flower on her chest,
like they saw her in her coffin
the last time.

What a long journey...
from earth to heaven;
and we can't say,
I do not want to go,
nor even
I want to go see my town,
my friends,

a casa unni nascivu,
a fossa ...
a cinniri.

Chi vinnimu a fari nno munnu
si nascemu pi mòriri?

5 ottobre 1980

the house where I was born,
the grave…
the ashes.

What did we come to do on earth,
if we were born to die?

October 5, 1980

About the Author

Ignazio Buttitta was born on 19 September 1899 in Bagheria (Palermo). Self-taught, he had various trades: butcher's boy, delicatessen, food wholesaler, sales representative. On October 15, 1922, on the eve of the March on Rome he led a popular revolt in his town. In the same year he founded the "Filippo Turati" cultural circle, which published the weekly paper "The poor people." Until 1928 he was co-director of the monthly Palermo dialect publication "La Trazzera," suppressed by fascism. After publishing Sintimintali (1923) and the poem Marabedda (1928) the poet officially kept silent, but his poems continued to circulate clandestinely.

His first anti-fascist poem was published in 1944 in the second issue of "Rinascita." Buttitta began to publish his works again only in 1954, with *Lu pani si chiama pani*, which gave him international fame.

In 1943 Bagheria had been bombed and Buttitta, to distance the family from the dangers of war, moved to Codogno (Milan). He believed he could return to Sicily alone, but the Allied landing prevented him from crossing the Strait of Messina. During his stay in Lombardy Buttitta participated in the clandestine struggle and was arrested twice by the fascists. When, after the Liberation, he returned to Sicily, he found his food warehouses looted. In order to live (he already had four children) he was forced to return to Lombardy and to undertake the activity of trade representative.

This was an important period of study for the poet, who was able to meet and frequent Quasimodo and Vittorini almost every evening. In 1960 he settled permanently in Bagheria. He purchased a house in Aspra facing the sea where he lived for the rest of his life. From that time forward he was finally able to devote himself to poetry with greater serenity, thus realizing his old dream. His house became a meeting place for people who came to see him from all over the world. He passed away on April 5th 1997. He was 97 years old.

Bibliography

Books published by Ignazio Buttitta

Buttitta Ignazio, *Sintimintali*, Palermo 1923.
Buttitta Ignazio, *Marabedda*, Edizione La Trazzera, Palermo 1927.
Buttitta Ignazio, *Lu pani si chiama pani*, Edizioni di Cultura Sociale, Roma 1954.
Buttitta Ignazio, *LU TRENU DI LU SULI IL TRENO DEL SOLE / La vera storia di SALVATORE GIULIANO*, Introduzione polemica di Leonardo Sciascia, Edizioni Avanti 1963.
Buttitta Ignazio, *La paglia bruciata*, Feltrinelli Editore, Milano 1968.
Buttitta Ignazio, *Io faccio il poeta*, Feltrinelli Editore, Milano 1972.
Buttitta Ignazio, *Il poeta in piazza*, Feltrinelli Editore, Milano 1974.
Buttitta Ignazio, *Lu curtigghiu di li Raunisi*, Editore Niccolò Giannotta, Catania 1975.
Buttitta Ignazio, *Pietre nere*, Feltrinelli Editore, Milano 1983.
Buttitta Ignazio, *Lu pani si chiama pani*, Palermo 1999.
Buttitta Ignazio, *La peddi nova*, Sellerio Editore, Palermo 2013.

Critical Works on Buttitta

Ancona Rosa Maria (a cura di), *Ignazio Buttitta. Profilo di poeta in elzeviro*, Collana Thalìa 1989.
Ancona Rosa Maria, *Ignazio Buttitta*, Edizione Thalìa 2014.
Beccaria Gian Luigi, *Le orme della parola*, Editore Rizzoli, Milano 2013.
Calì Santo, *La notti longa*, volume primo, Centro Studi Santo Calì, Linguaglossa 1972.
Camilleri Salvatore (a cura di), *Poeti Siciliani Contemporanei*, Edizioni Arte e Folklore di Sicilia, Catania 1979.
Di Marco Salvatore, *La questione della koinè e la poesia dialettale siciliana*, Edizioni I Quaderni del giornale di poesia siciliana, Palermo 1995.
Di Marco Salvatore, *Il filo dell'aquilone. Saggi su Ignazio Buttitta*, Nuova IPSA editore, Palermo 2000.
Di Marco Salvatore, *Sulle alte cime delle querce. Ignazio Buttitta dagli esordi a Marabedda e oltre*, Annali della Facoltà di Lettere e Filosofia dell'Università di Palermo, Palermo 2003.
Di Marco Salvatore (a cura di), *Il cantiere della lingua madre*, Agrigento 2006.
Di Marco Salvatore, *Discorsi brevi sulla poesia*, Accademia di studi "Cielo D'Alcamo" 2009.
Di Marco Salvatore, *Il versante dialettale. Saggi di letteratura siciliana*, Nuova Ipsa Editore, Palermo 2010.
Di Marco Salvatore, *Gli occhi del mondo. Saggi su Ignazio Buttitta*, Coppola editore 2011.
Di Marco Salvatore (a cura di), *Giornale di poesia siciliana*, Palermo 1988 - 2008.
Lo Bianco Nicola, *I tempi del poeta in piazza. Omaggio a Ignazio Buttitta*, Edizioni La Zisa 2013.

Monaco Lorenzo (a cura di), *Ignazio Buttitta. Cultura è Libertà*, Salemi (TP) 2012.
Nuove Effemeridi, Anno X n°39, Ignazio Buttitta. Edizioni Guida, Palermo 1997.
Piraino Raffaello, *L'airone bianco e altri racconti*, Coppola editore 2009.
Puglisi Marta (a cura di), *Prime e nuovissime*, Gruppo Editoriale Forma, Torino 1983.
Puleo Carlo, *Ignazio Buttitta, il presente della memoria. 100 foto e 18 racconti*. ISSPE Palermo 2016.
Quaderni di Studi Digiovannei, numero 2 febbraio 2004, Istituzione Culturale "Alessio Di Giovanni", Cianciana (AG).
Scalabrino, Marco, *Ignazio Buttitta: dalla piazza all'universo,* Venezia: Edizione dell'autrice, 2019.
Scardina Maura Maria, *U dialettu è a lingua di patri*. Ignazio Buttitta. la voce di un poeta comune. Università di Bologna. Tesi di laurea Anno Accademico 2017-2018.
Tedesco Natale, *Ignazio Buttitta e il mondo popolare siciliano,* Flaccovio Editore, Palermo 1965.
Zagarella Maria Nivea, Quelle "Pietre Nere" dalle piaghe sempre aperte e Ignazio Buttitta e un rinvenimento d'archivio, in *Tra Rigore e Passione, Interventi di critica militante*, Bonanno Editore, Acireale - Roma 2018.